Rescue publication number 4

The Future of London's Past

a survey of the archaeological
implications of planning and development
in the nation's capital

Rescue publications

1 David Leigh (ed.), *First Aid for Finds* (Southampton 1972).
   50p (members of *Rescue*, 40p).

2 John Williams (ed.), *The Northampton-Wellingborough
   Expressway: an archaeological survey* (Worcester 1973).
   30p (members of *Rescue*, 20p).

3 H. Barnie and D. Robinson, *The North Wales Shell
   Pipeline: an archaeological survey* (Worcester 1973).
   40p (members of *Rescue*, 30p).

4 Martin Biddle and Daphne M. Hudson with Carolyn M.
   Heighway, *The Future of London's Past: a survey of the
   archaeological implications of planning and development in the
   nation's capital* (Worcester 1973).
   £3·50 (members of *Rescue*, £2·50).

Obtainable post-free from *Rescue*, 25a The Tything,
Worcester.

THE CITY FROM THE AIR
showing the wall and the position of London Bridge, 1176–1831
Fox Photos Ltd.

The Future of London's Past

a survey of the archaeological
implications of planning and
development in the nation's capital

Martin Biddle

and

Daphne M. Hudson

with Carolyn M. Heighway

Rescue
a trust for British Archaeology
Worcester

First published 1973
by Rescue: a trust for British archaeology
25a The Tything, Worcester

Printed in Great Britain by Lund Humphries

For
Professor W. F. (Peter) Grimes
who in the years from 1946 to 1962
greatly advanced the study of
London's past

Haec est regia illa totius Angliae civitas LONDINUM . . .
multarum gentium commertio nobilitata, exculta domibus,
ornata templis, excelsa arcibus, claris ingeniis, viris omnium
artium doctrinarumque genere praestantibus, percelebris.

Braun and Hogenberg, 1572

. . . the history of archaeology in the City of London recalls the
story of the Sibylline Books. Knowledge is offered to each
generation at a price – and is destroyed when the price is not
paid. The price rises for each generation . . . and the remaining
store of information diminishes. None has yet been prepared
to pay in full . . . If ever a generation arises that is prepared
to pay the full price of a total scientific excavation over
whatever area is then available, complete pages of the Book
will be won. But by that time very few pages indeed will
remain.

Ralph Merrifield, 1965

Preface

by

Sir Mortimer Wheeler, CH, CIE, MC, TD, FRS, FBA, HON.V-PSA

It is with unusual pleasure that I accept Mr Biddle's invitation to introduce this timely – indeed, desperately urgent – book on *The Future of London's Past*. Without any periphrastic fumbling I hail it bluntly as a brilliant survey of deeds and needs. If I can claim any right to do so, I can seek justification, I suppose, only in personal terms. When in 1926 I deliberately cut short a comfortable and predictable career as Director of the National Museum of Wales and returned to London, I did so with a definite plan not only in my mind but actually in my pocket. It was a scheme for the foundation of an active archaeological research institution within the University of London, the first comprehensive scheme of its kind in the country. And the first practical step was to discover a focal sanctuary in London where my plans could assume shape and context. Chance presented just such a sanctuary at the London Museum, where in July 1926 I took up my working abode amidst the alien disjecta of modern ceremonial and the dusty curios of tip-heaps and junk-shops.

There, as Martin Biddle has been good enough to recall, quickly sprang into existence a sort of small-scale research institution, which provided lectures to conscripted University of London students and an unrestricted home for a miscellaneous group of young men and women (notably G. C. Dunning, Frank Cottrill and Eric Birley) who shared their special studies with the day-by-day examination of building-excavations within the London area. The London Museum had in effect become overnight something very like a shelter for nomadic research, primarily on London itself, but secondarily on the whole range of the tidal Thames which was then still yielding varied archaeological material under the impact of residual dredging.

I would for a moment emphasize this duality of of purpose and direction although as a matter of urgency it is now substantially out of date. Ob-viously the supervision of building-sites was then as now by far the highest priority. The old bed of the river, once so productive, was by that time approaching almost complete erosion. Nevertheless it still demanded a measure of organized vigilance. This was brought home to me in 1927 when as a collateral activity I undertook the introduction and lay-out of the *Roman London* volume of the Royal Commission on Historical Monuments (England). Why were *Londinium* and its successors sited and shaped as they were? Answers to this and attendant problems compelled continuing and widespread environmental study.

One or two examples. 'Information received' in 1926–7 led me on more than one occasion, with a sack upon my back, across the desert flats below Tilbury, where riverside dykes confined London's stinking rubbish, dumped daily in steaming masses at low level and infested by rats of fearsome aspect. My goal was the northern foreshore of the river where, at a depth of 13 feet and upwards vertically below Trinity High Water, the receding tide re-vealed circular daub-and-wattle huts, and a great spread of Roman and Romano-Belgic pottery stretched for 200 yards beneath a fluctuating canopy of tide and tidal mud. Combined with other factors, the submerged Tilbury huts began to produce a new picture of the Thames estuary in relation to riparian occupation and tidal flow in Roman times.

Within a few months of the Tilbury episode the patronage of a metropolitan newspaper enabled us to uncover comparable phenomena some miles up-stream at the ancient Brentford crossing. But what-ever the contribution of these opportunist probings to a developing reconstruction of the London environment, it was already beyond doubt in the 'twenties that the real focus of concern lay within the half-mile above and below London Bridge in its variable embodiments. Hereabouts, it would appear, was the tide-head of two thousand years ago;

indeed, perhaps much later if we may enlarge the Anglo-Saxon Chronicle's assurance that in 1114 'men went riding or walking over the Thames eastward of London Bridge'. And before 1930, as I have said, a handful of whole-time observers was hard at work in this central area. Their resources were wretchedly inadequate, but already before the Second World War they had become a recognized feature of the London scene.

Circumstance involved me professionally in the blitz of 1940, but it was not until the end of 1943 that a brief return from overseas enabled me to envisage in a more forward-looking sense something of the nature and immensity of the salvage problem – in every implication of the term – which was still accumulating almost day by day. A hundred acres or more of ruthless devastation included more than half of the western of the two hills upon which London is built, and whole stretches of Thames-side . . . The situation need not be particularized (there is a provisional map in *Antiquity* for September 1944). But already there were hopeful stirrings of public interest. What was then the Office of Works, through its active Chief Inspector of Ancient Monuments, Bryan St.John O'Neil, was doing with a good heart what little it could do in recovery and general aid. And, more reluctantly, the City authorities were slowly becoming aware of the long-term existence of a salvage problem. Nevertheless with hindsight it is easy to see how inadequately

planned the whole situation not unnaturally was at this time. The national consciousness had not yet been sufficiently attuned to historical and archaeological thinking; and there was no over-all mind of sufficient stature to point the way.

Thirty years later the position has changed and is still changing. It is now proper, if not yet universal, for any town or city in the country with a proud past to exhibit that pride in terms of more or less systematic restitution. The machinery set up locally for this purpose is on varying scales and of unequal efficiency. But experience has been assembled, and cities such as Winchester, Oxford, York, and half-a dozen others can claim to have demonstrated how the thing should be done. There still remains the greatest city of them all.

The task facing a commensurate London Archaeological Unit such as is displayed in the present charter – for such it may fairly be designated – is here faultlessly elaborated in terms of motives, manpower and method, based upon widespread and detailed experience under the leadership of those best qualified to undertake it. Its monetary demands are necessarily considerable; its outcome in terms of new knowledge of the city which is after all our greatest civic artefact lies beyond the pale of doubt. It is for me an honour to acclaim its founders, Martin Biddle and his colleagues, and to wish them godspeed upon their URGENT work of Rescue.

Mortimer Wheeler

Contents

Figures in the text

(All at a scale of 1:20,000, unless otherwise shown)

Maps in the case

(All at a scale of 1:5,000, Maps 2–8 forming transparent overlays to Map 1)

For the sources of the maps and figures, see Appendix II, p.75

Acknowledgements

The chief officers and staffs of various departments of the Corporation of the City of London and the Greater London Council must be named first among those who have willingly and fully answered our many requests for the information required in the compilation of this survey: the Department of Architecture and Planning (Research Section and Civic Design Setion), the City Engineer's Department, Guildhall Library, Guildhall Library Print Room, and Guildhall Museum of the Corporation; and the Department of Planning and Transportation (Intelligence Section) of the Greater London Council. It is proper that we should make special mention of Guildhall Museum, its Director Mr Max Hebditch, its Assistant Director Mr Ralph Merrifield, and their staff, particularly Mr Hugh Chapman and Mr John Clark, for the scholarly care with which they have dealt with all our professional inquiries.

Everyone who writes on the history of London is indebted beyond adequate expression to the host of scholars whose work is the foundation of present-day knowledge of the City: if the structure we have erected is not always that which those who laid these foundations might have expected, this is frequently because their own work has contributed greatly to the changes that have taken place. The importance of their work is but inadequately reflected in our bibliography (Appendix III, p.77), and in the many references to it.

Among those others who have helped us from their own knowledge of London we should like to thank Mr Graham Dawson, Mr Nicholas Farrant, Mrs Gillian Keir and Dr J. P. C. Kent. We have received valuable practical assistance from Mr F. G. Aldsworth, Messrs Chas. E. Goad Ltd, Mr Nicholas Griffiths, Mr R. J. Kiln, and Miss Caroline Raison. The illustrations were prepared by Studio Briggs under the supervision of Mr Alan Hollingbery and the maps were drawn by Miss Coral Mula. We wish particularly to thank our printers, Lund Humphries, and especially Mr J. A. de Fonblanque, for the care they have taken and the good advice they have offered at all stages of the production.

The preparation of a survey of this kind is a costly matter. *Rescue* is extremely grateful to Mr R. J. Kiln and Mr G. A. P. Thomas for guarantees which allowed the work to proceed, and to the following for generous financial contributions which have ensured its publication: the Corporation of the City of London, through Guildhall Museum (towards the cost of the maps); the *Sunday Times*; visitors to the Wandsworth Historical Society's 1972 rescue excavations; and many firms and public bodies in the City of London.

Martin Biddle, *Winchester Research Unit*
Daphne M. Hudson, *Department of Civic Design, University of Liverpool*
Carolyn M. Heighway, *Council for British Archaeology*

1 Introduction

1.1   The purpose of this survey is twofold. It attempts to assess the current state of archaeological knowledge about the City of London in relation to the destruction of the evidence by redevelopment and to suggest a solution whereby a great deal more could be investigated and recorded than is at present possible. It also provides in a series of eight maps the means of making an outline assessment of the archaeological potential of any site in the City and offers in an appendix a schedule of the sites to be developed in the immediate future, and in the next five years, with brief comments on their archaeological possibilities.

1.2   We have tried to take a positive rather than a negative view of the City's archaeology. Too much has been lost in the past because the difficulties have seemed too great, because the potential of a site has not been fully evaluated beforehand, or because it was felt that existing cellars would already have done too much damage to make further investigation worthwhile. Much has been lost, but it is better to observe a site in hope and waste a visit, than to omit a visit and fail to record evidence that was then available but now no longer exists. For this reason the schedule in Appendix I has tended to take an optimistic rather than a pessimistic view of the potential of the sites it lists.

1.3   We have tried also to approach the whole problem from an archaeological point of view rather than in terms of the passing opportunity offered by the development of one site or another. Rather than list the available sites in categories of supposed descending archaeological importance, we have preferred to establish first the archaeological and historical priorities and then to see which sites offered the chance of obtaining new information. By thus taking the rescue problem by the scruff of the neck, as it were, we have sought to force out of it a programme of research. Recognizing that in any realistic world resources will only be available, even on the scale suggested in these pages, to investigate thoroughly a proportion of the threatened sites, we have felt that the examination of these sites must

form part of a planned and not an opportunist programme.

1.4   Although this survey is concerned principally with the archaeology of the City of London – and in our text 'City' means the modern administrative county of the City of London, while 'city' or 'London', suitably qualified, refers usually to one or other of its former periods – it must be obvious that the study of this more limited area cannot at all be divorced from the study of a much wider hinterland, covering most of the Greater London Council area. For no period is this more true than for the fifth to seventh centuries A.D., as we stress elsewhere. Whether this should be taken as an argument for one archaeological service covering both the City and the GLC area is perhaps uncertain. The City presents a distinct research problem, a distinction heightened by the difficulties surrounding its investigation, which perhaps outweigh even the physical and administrative problems confronting archaeology in the larger area around. If there were to be a unified regional service for the whole of Greater London, it is certain that it would have to include a separate division for the City.

1.5   A few words on the use of this survey may be appropriate. Cross-references to chapters and paragraphs are given in the form (4.41); text references to the bibliography in Appendix III are preceded by an italic figure referring to the numbered section of the bibliography where the work will be found alphabetically listed, e.g. 11. Grimes 1968 will be found in Appendix III, section 11, under 'G'.

1.6   The maps are designed as a working tool. Hence they are provided loose and at the same scale. Maps 2–8 are printed on transparent paper so that they may be laid over one another in any order to produce the required combination of information, and at the same time related to a base map, Map 1, reproduced from the Ordnance Survey. Thus Map 2, showing Roman London, can be read over Map 5, showing existing basements, to obtain an idea of the areas still available for investigation, and their significance in relation to Roman London. A similar combination of *Maps 5* and *8* would show the extent to which future development sites had already been archaeologically destroyed. Combination of *Maps 2* and *3* or *Maps 3* and *4* would make it possible to follow the effect of one period's topography on that of a succeeding age. These maps can be kept up to date by the addition of new information, or could be entirely redrawn, as necessary, with *Map 1* serving as a base. Planning information changes constantly. We are aware that changes have already occurred since the maps were proofed. We are also aware of the shortcomings of the information that was sometimes available, and we comment below on the difficulties in relation to *Map 5*, for example (*5.5*). These maps should nevertheless remain serviceable for some time, although the early obsolescence of *Maps 2–4* must be eagerly awaited, as a sign that new information is available about London's past.

1.7   The solution we have outlined here in *Chapter 7* presents one possible answer to the serious plight in which the archaeology of the City now stands. Other solutions may differ in detail, or even more substantially, especially in matters of organization, or over the location of the ultimate responsibility for the work which must be done. But long experience and some familiarity with the nature of these problems throughout the country has convinced us that the scale of our solution, large as it may seem, is dictated by the facts of the situation as set out in *Chapters 3 to 6*. These chapters lead directly to the solution proposed, and thus to the financial implications discussed in *7.16–23*. Great as these are in absolute terms, they are not, given the size and state of London's archaeology, out of scale with what has already been accepted as realistic in some other towns and cities.

1.8   One matter has not been included, namely the architectural recording of standing buildings threatened with demolition. In the City of London almost all these buildings are of post-medieval date. Their recording requires a specifically architectural approach, and often an understanding of industrial archaeology as well. It may be felt, perhaps rightly, that this recording should also be entrusted to a City archaeological unit. It might also be considered, with equal reason, that it should be a function of the Department of Architecture and Planning of the Corporation. Whatever may be decided – and it would be a simple matter to include a small architectural team in a City archaeological unit – it is urgent that the need for this recording should be widely appreciated. Photographs are not sufficient. Measured drawings, plans, sections, and elevations are essential to any adequate understanding of these complex buildings that served an empire's trade. It is a task for professionals, a task that is not at present usually undertaken, even in the case of listed buildings.

2 Summary

2.1   Antiquities dug from the soil of London have attracted the interest and enthusiasm of antiquaries for several centuries. About seventy years ago a conscious effort began to extract from such finds, and from the observation of buried structures, some connected account of the origins and early development of the City. This work, prosecuted with renewed vigour in the aftermath of World War II, has never kept pace with the destruction, of the very evidence being sought, by the necessary but relentless erection of modern buildings. Official concern has been little stirred; archaeologists have rarely left their trenches for the platform of public debate.

2.2   As an archaeological site the City of London is extremely large and, having been occupied for some two thousand years, the deposits laid down by its past inhabitants are exceptionally thick. Most attention has been concentrated so far on its Roman past, and little effort has been devoted to the investigation of the Anglo-Saxon period, when the modern city was born.

2.3   Although one quarter of the City's area has already been destroyed in archaeological terms, and over a half at least partially damaged, major problems still remain relating to every aspect and period of the City's Roman, Anglo-Saxon and medieval past. Many of these problems can still be solved – by unprecedented effort and expenditure – but only twenty years at most remain in which this work can be done. By then, and more likely by the later 1980s, the remaining archaeological deposits will have been almost entirely destroyed by the increasing tempo and intensity of redevelopment.

2.4   The solution suggested by experience in other towns and cities is the establishment of a City of London Archaeological Unit, perhaps as an independent body, possibly as a division of the new Museum of London. Such a unit would be designed to excavate, observe and record threatened archaeological sites throughout the City and to publish its results. Its annual budget might be of the order of £185,000 at full complement, and its expenditure over the next ten years might approach £2 million.

Its success requires the establishment of close working relationships with development and business interests in an atmosphere of mutual confidence and co-operation, and against a background of good archaeological legislation protecting the interests of both sides.

3 The growth of archaeological research in the City

3.1   Interest in the material remains of London's past can be said to fall into five main periods. The era of antiquarian curiosity lasted from the end of the sixteenth until the early years of the nineteenth century. It was followed by the more precise concern of a small band of Victorian and Edwardian scholars whose work was often enhanced by the highly professional standards of architectural recording characteristic of their age. Although interrupted by the First World War, this phase lasted into the 1920s, when it gave way to a decade of synthesis of existing knowledge which will always be associated with the name of Sir Mortimer Wheeler. This was also the period when the first professional observers were at work recording the archaeological evidence revealed during building construction. The Second World War brought this third stage to a close and through the immense destruction wrought by aerial bombardment posed problems and offered opportunities for archaeological research on a scale never before envisaged (*fig.1*). In the years which followed, Professor W. F. Grimes inaugurated a new phase in the study of London's archaeology on the basis of properly conducted and carefully recorded excavations. At the same time permanent arrangements were made for the observation of building sites. The achievements of these years were great. When they ended in 1962 it seemed for a brief moment as if there was no future for London's past, as if all hope of recovering further knowledge in advance of redevelopment had gone. These fears were almost at once dispelled by a series of remarkable discoveries during the sixties, and by the increasing importance of the contribution made by volunteer workers to the solution of some of the practical problems of manpower and organization. This fresh activity has taken place against the accelerating tempo of redevelopment: not now the opportunities presented by bombed sites, but rather those offered by the sites of buildings which survived war-time attack to end their useful life in the new world of the sixties and seventies. With the scale of these works archaeology as now organized in the City cannot keep pace. It has neither the personnel nor the administration, neither the legal backing nor the finance. This fifth period of investigation into London's past has been a period of disarray.

3.2   The history of the investigation of Roman London has been admirably described down to 1964 by Ralph Merrifield (*3*. Merrifield 1965, 1–28). No general account has yet been written about the investigation of later periods, perhaps because so little has yet been achieved by comparison with work on Roman London that no useful account can be compiled (*fig.4*). The background to this survey requires, however, at least an outline of the administrative arrangements behind the development of London's archaeology since the First World War, and some indication of the principal events.

Archaeology in the City between the Wars

3.3   The Edwardian tradition of Philip Norman and F. W. Reader was maintained in the post-war years by Frank Lambert, Museum Clerk – as the curator of Guildhall Museum was then called – of the City of London Corporation. Lambert investigated building sites in 1919–21 and published his results, but with his departure from the Museum in 1924, it proved difficult to make any fully satisfactory arrangement, the Museum continuing to have a staff of one, Lambert's successor Quintin Waddington, to carry out all its growing tasks. New movements were afoot, however, signalled by the appointment of Dr R. E. M. (*now* Sir Mortimer) Wheeler as Keeper of the London Museum in 1926.

3.4   Wheeler's new post heralded ten years of review and consolidation in the archaeology of London. At this time modern methods of archaeological study had scarcely been applied to the objects found in the City, let alone to the sites of their discovery. Wheeler changed this situation in a series of London Museum Catalogues written mainly after work in the evenings: *London and the Vikings* appeared in 1927, *London in Roman Times* in 1930, and *London and the Saxons* in 1935. The first and third of these have still not been replaced, and their importance will be discussed later (*4.22*). *London in Roman Times* was in some sense the by-product of *Roman London*, published in 1928 as the third volume of the Royal Commission on Historical Monuments' London *Inventory*. Wheeler was again responsible, and the work has an enduring value as a

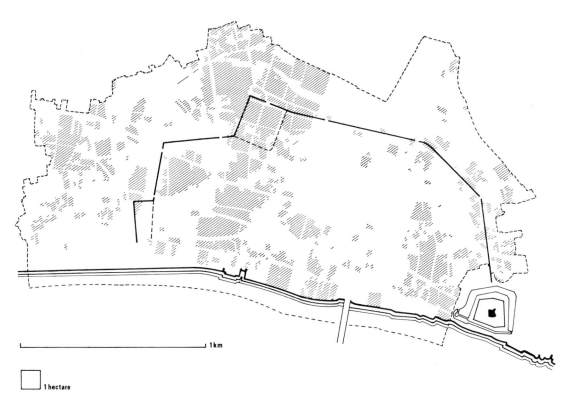

Fig.1 Areas of the City destroyed by enemy action, 1939–45 (1 : 20,000)

factual and fully referenced survey of all that was then known of the Roman city. It was much more than just a survey, however, for it contained an introduction of sixty-seven pages which with its blend of compressed synthesis and controlled hypothesis placed the study of Roman London on an entirely new footing.

3.5 Up to 1928 there was still no real solution to the problem of recording fresh evidence as it was exposed in contractors' excavations. In that year however, the Society of Antiquaries, exercising a positive attitude towards the archaeology of the nation's capital that had long been seen in the space provided in *Archaeologia* for the publication of reports on City discoveries, appointed the first of its professional Investigators of Building Excavations in London. The post was held in 1928–9 by E. B. Birley, in 1929–34 by G. C. Dunning, and lastly in 1934–7 by Frank Cottrill. The post then lapsed, and responsibility for recording reverted to Guildhall Museum, where Waddington was still single-handed until the appointment of Adrian Oswald as his assistant in 1939, on the eve of the Second World War.

3.6 The inter-war years saw the development of two trends that were to change the whole character of London's archaeology: the gradual acceptance of the need for professional staff to be responsible for investigation and recording, and the application of modern archaeological methods to the study of

the results. This latter trend was confirmed by G. C. Dunning's paper of 1945 on the 'Two fires of Roman London', in which the evidence of stratigraphy and of distributions was used to interpret the finds made in 1929–37 during his and Frank Cottrill's tenure of the post of Investigator of Building Excavations (*3.* Dunning 1945).

3.7 These same years did not see the application of controlled excavation to the solution of the problems of London's archaeology; nor did they see an increasing awareness of the role to be played by the Corporation. Indeed less was achieved by Guildhall staff in 1924–39 than during Lambert's tenure of 1914–24. The achievements of the twenties and thirties, which were very considerable, were the achievements of outside bodies: the Royal Commission, the Society of Antiquaries, and the London Museum.

Archaeology in the City 1945–62

3.8 About one-third of the ancient walled city was destroyed by enemy action in 1939–45 (*fig.1*). The archaeological opportunity presented by this grim harvest was recognized before the destruction was even complete. At the beginning of 1944, and on the eve of his departure for India, Mortimer Wheeler wrote in *Antiquity* of 'The Rebuilding of London', 'at stake is nearly two thousand years of accumulated material bearing upon the history and everyday life of the greatest city in the world, potential knowledge which can now be acquired for relatively modest cost but can never again be bought' (*9*. Wheeler 1944, 152). The nettles were grasped with some degree of caution. In May 1944 the newly-founded Council for British Archaeology requested the Society of Antiquaries to take action. In April 1945 the Society set up a Committee which endeavoured to recruit the support of the City Corporation, which eventually allowed its Librarian to sit on the Committee. The then Ministry of Works gave strong support and were indeed to be the bastion and support of the whole future effort. In November 1945 the Committee appointed W. F. Grimes to be its supervisor of excavations, and a trial excavation took place the following spring. Fifteen months later in July 1947 an enlarged body held its first Annual General Meeting. There followed sixteen years of unremitting labour which brought to the problems of London's archaeology for the first time the analytical power of scientific excavation under the control of one of its most skilled practitioners. Professor Grimes has himself summarized the results of this work in a book published in 1968 that has become a classic of urban archaeology (*11*. Grimes 1968).

3.9   The years 1945–62 hold many lessons for the future of archaeology in London. Many of these points Grimes has made himself (*11*. Grimes 1968, 218–41), but in view of the difficulties of the last few years they can bear resatting and even some addition. The Committee was originally to be called 'The Roman London Excavation Committee', a restrictive title that was soon changed to 'The Roman and Mediaeval London Excavation Council'. Grimes's book reflects this extended range and contains much of the greatest interest regarding the later periods. Nevertheless the lure of Roman antiquity can today still tend to outweigh other considerations, particularly when on any given site it is easy – if not always correct – to assume the destruction of the later levels. The lack of balance in the present state of knowledge and research is serious (*fig.4*).

3.10   Over £40,000 was spent in the years 1946–62, an average of about £2,600 a year. This sum represented what could be obtained, and not what was actually needed. It took no account of inflation and rising wages (labourers earned £6 a week in 1949, £12 in 1960); it did not allow the use of plant (although problems of soil movement and disposal conditioned both what and how much could be done on every site); it left the Director virtually single-handed until 1953; it allowed very little provision towards the preparation of the immensely complex final reports which, as British archaeology slowly learns (*14*. Frere 1972, 2–3), cannot be compiled by the lone unaided scholar. It is not surprising in these circumstances that the final reports have not yet appeared; it is remarkable that we have

so full an account as *The Excavation of Roman and Mediaeval London*.

3.11   The sources of all grants over £100 were as follows (*11*. Grimes 1968, 245–51).

	£
H.M. Government	26,300
Bank of England	2,750
Anonymous	2,000
L.C.C.	2,000
Other banks (5)	1,968
Business and finance houses (12)	1,501
St Bride's Church	1,050
Livery companies (4)	700
Private individuals and a trust (4)	550
Corporation of London	550
Society of Antiquaries	350
National Geographic Society	210
	39,929
There were 481 other gifts of between £1 and £96	3,570
	£43,499

The situation is clear enough: a national awareness of the problem is reflected in the Government contribution, contrasted with extreme reluctance in the City. The City Corporation's own contribution of £550 represents less than £40 a year, or 1·3% of the whole excavation budget for 1946–62. This figure does not stand alone. Seventeen banks and twenty-one livery companies gave grants of less than £50.

3.12   Finance on this scale left no margin for administration, and this must partly explain both the general decision not to employ volunteer labour (*11*. Grimes 1968, 225–7), and the virtual absence of public relations. The latter reacted in turn – for the whole is a vicious cycle – both on the general ability of the Excavation Council to attract large-scale funds, and on the generosity of the public when at last its interest was aroused. Over 30,000 probably saw the Mithras temple site during one week in September 1954. They contributed about £250, less than 1p a head (*11*. Grimes 1968, 236). There is no room for criticism here, for the conditions of British archaeology in the mid-fifties cannot be compared with today. But there are obvious lessons, made all the more immediate by the problems raised by the Baynard Castle site early in 1972. Public relations are a duty when the public pays the cost of archaeology, whether as tax-payers or as rate-payers. Public relations are also vital to an activity like archaeology which is in competition with many other perhaps conflicting interests. Good public relations bring ample rewards – in cash, in assistance of every kind, and not least in the status of archaeological activities in the public realm of local and national government.

3.13 Shortage of cash and of bargaining power, and the decision to use only paid labour, conditioned the whole shape of the excavations of 1946–62. The aim was to try to excavate at least one trench on every available site, thus providing archaeologists with a properly recorded section of the archaeological deposits in as many places as possible throughout the City. There was the hope too, although never actually realized, that carefully positioned trenches might give an almost continuous cross-section through the ancient levels of London from north to south through the heart of the bomb-damaged area from Cripplegate to the Thames (*fig.1*). There can be no doubt that this was the right approach for the first stage of the operations. These were the first controlled excavations in the City, and there was almost everything to learn. Unfortunately the essential second stage, that of area excavations, was never reached. The limited resources available made it impossible. Even the trenches of the first stage had usually to be cut one after another through the years, for there was simply not enough money and not enough skilled supervision to do more.

3.14 The credit for achieving anything in these circumstances – and a great deal *was* achieved – belongs entirely to Professor Grimes, as the dedication of this survey implies, and to the members of the Excavation Council. The part played by the then Ministry of Works was the foundation of this achievement, and the generosity of the Trustees of the London Museum in allowing their Keeper to serve as director of excavations was its corner-stone. It is entirely understandable, however, that the appalling difficulties he had had to face led Professor Grimes in 1968 to take a despondent attitude towards the future of archaeology in the City of London (*11.* Grimes 1968, 218–9). Although the sixties may well appear in relation to the rapid evolution of British archaeology in general, to have been an unsatisfactory period in the development of archaeology in London, the outlines of a new approach were in fact already being laid and important new discoveries were taking place during the writing of Grimes's book.

3.15 Meanwhile there had been another development of exceptional importance. While the Excavation Council carried out meticulous controlled excavations on sites where rebuilding had not yet begun, other sites were being archaeologically destroyed by reconstruction. To record as much of the archaeology of these sites as was possible the City Corporation in 1949 appointed to the staff of Guildhall Museum its first full-time excavation assistant. Although the successive holders of this

post have usually been without formal training in archaeology, they have strengthened the old tradition of building-site investigation in the City, and have recovered a great deal that would otherwise have been entirely lost. But with many sites being redeveloped simultaneously, on a scale and at a rate (due to the use of modern machinery) never before encountered, it cannot be supposed that one person was able to give every site the constant or at least repeated attention such observation requires if it is to be fully productive in archaeological terms. Nor did this pressure allow time for publication of the results, except in short interim notes. The other disturbing implication of these appointments was the tacit assumption that observation of this kind, carried out under appalling conditions, with the evidence available only in part and often for a very short time (frequently a matter of minutes, rather than hours), could be entrusted to junior untrained staff. It is an assumption that has been widely made in British archaeology. In reality the observation and recording of the fragmentary evidence revealed on building sites requires a high degree of knowledge, skill, and experience. Only those who have been trained over several years on major excavations dealing with a wide variety of sites and covering the main historical periods should be entrusted with this work. On their skill depends the sole possible record and on-site interpretation of evidence that is never seen in its entirety, or except under conditions of considerable physical stress, of noise and mud, and even personal danger.

Archaeology in the City 1963–72

3.16 Excavations carried out by the Roman and Mediaeval London Excavation Council were concluded in 1962. This was a period when the rebuilding of the City after war-time destruction was coming to an end. The redevelopment of sites which had escaped damage by bombing was by contrast just beginning. No new arrangements were made to deal with the changed situation, although the activities of Guildhall Museum's excavation assistant continued and were indeed intensified. Regular short reports on the work of 1960–70 were contributed annually to the *Transactions of the London and Middlesex Archaeological Society*. These arrangements could not cope, however, with the rapidly increasing tempo of rebuilding (*5.12*). Quite apart from the steady loss of information due to the impossibility of keeping an eye on so many simultaneous projects, major crises were bound to occur. The discovery of the Huggin Hill bath-house in 1964 led to the immediate need for amateur volunteers, by whose help a considerable area was excavated. Volunteers had at last appeared to stay, and in October 1964 formed themselves into the City of London Excavation Group, now the City of London Archaeological Society. Under the direction of Guildhall Museum's excavation assistant, P. R. V. Marsden, volunteer work continued, notably on the Roman 'palace' in 1964–6 and on the Coal Exchange bath-house in 1968. Even this degree of volunteer support could not cope with the major problems presented by development on part of the forum site at the end of 1968. In default of adequate permanent arrangements geared to this kind of situation, and faced with an incessant day-round activity which was beyond the resources of the Excavation Group, help had to be called in from outside and was provided by Brian Philp and the CIB Rescue Corps from Kent. The results were impressive, if still unpublished, and a vivid demonstration of how much can still remain to be discovered. The then Ministry of Public Building and Works also undertook some excavations, notably at the Tower in 1957 and 1963, and during the consolidation of the city wall to the north.

3.17   Much was done in these years, but everything was on an *ad hoc* basis. A site could lie open for months while the owner refused permission for excavation, presumably fearing the effect on his negotiations for sale. On sites where permission for excavation was given, it might extend only to the period of a public holiday, perhaps three days. The Kent team on the forum, invited to leave after nine days' work, remained for ninety without endangering the construction schedule. Conditions on sites owned by the Corporation were much better, as might be expected, but even today it is rare to get reasonable access, often any access at all, to privately-owned developments. The fear of another Mithras, and greatly exaggerated rumours of how much that delay had cost the developer (it was actually about £4,000) were and perhaps still are a considerable factor in the essentially reluctant attitude of most private developers. Many of the difficulties are undoubtedly of archaeology's own making. There is no evidence to suggest that realistic budgets for archaeology in the City were ever composed until 1972, and certainly there was no demand from the archaeological world at large that they should be. Not until 1972 when archaeologists spoke out publicly against the inadequate investigation of the Baynard Castle site was there any open dissent from the general acceptance of how things were. If archaeologists were prepared to accept the situation, it is hard to see why developers should have taken them seriously. They still do not do so: at the time of writing (January 1973) one of the largest developers in the City has just explained his reluctance to allow Guildhall Museum time for an adequate investigation on the grounds that 'we do not know who these people are, and do not want just anyone coming on to our site to delay work'. Unfair as this may be to Guildhall Museum, such remarks are an all too common result of archaeology's failure to achieve professional recognition in the workaday world.

3.18   The sixties did, however, see important advances in our understanding of Roman London as a result of two books published by the Assistant Director of Guildhall Museum, Ralph Merrifield. Forty years after the Royal Commission volume of 1928 and Wheeler's London Museum Catalogue of 1930 (*3.4*), the current state of knowledge was summarized in *The Roman City of London* (*3*. Merrifield 1965) and *Roman London* (*3*. Merrifield 1969). These books, especially the former, provide the essential basis for further work. It is only to be regretted that no-one has yet attempted the same task for the later periods. But these years did also see the publication of Grimes's account of the work of 1946–62 (*11*. Grimes 1968), and the foundation of a new journal *The London Archaeologist*.

3.19   The sixties were thus a time of change in London archaeology. The importance of the contribution to be made by volunteers was fully recognized. With the increased labour thus available, area excavations were undertaken for the first time. These years were also a period of synthesis with a series of general publications no other city can rival (*3.18*). But London did not share in the general advance of urban archaeology. No improvements can be recorded in the financial provision for London's archaeology at this time, nor in the organization or administration of its activities. There was no solution to the problem of preparing for full publication the immense back-log of previous work. Most serious of all, there was no discernible reaction to the increasing rate of development (*5.12*), and no attempt to improve the status of archaeology in the City, to make its voice more strongly and more responsibly heard. These faults cannot be laid at the door of Guildhall Museum or its staff, for they were in every sense a failure of British archaeology as a whole. When at last a general opinion was voiced in the spring of 1972, the City Corporation was not slow to react. The following summer saw the most extensive programme of excavations yet carried out in one season by Guildhall Museum. Budgets have been substantially increased, with the Department of the Environment playing a characteristically vital role. There seems now every hope for the future, especially at the moment when the new Museum of London is about to emerge from the amalgamation of the Guildhall and London Museums, the two institutions which have in the past achieved so much of what has actually been done in the archaeology of the City.

4 The current state of knowledge

The range and scale of the problem

4.1   There is general agreement that permanent settlement on the site of London began with the events of A.D.43. No evidence for other than transitory occupation during the prehistoric period has ever come to light, and the imported Arretine pottery once thought to be evidence of pre-Roman settlement must now be seen as part of the evidence for the earliest phases of the Roman presence.

4.2   The site of London was probably never afterwards deserted. It may never even have entirely lost its urban character, for it is the one town of Roman Britain, with the possible exception of York, where urban conditions may have continued unbroken between the end of the fourth century and the beginning of the eighth (4.24–9). Whatever the nature of London during this period, there is ample archaeological evidence of the intensity of occupation throughout nearly four centuries of Roman rule, and sufficient evidence from documentary sources and comparative studies to show that the late Saxon city was of very considerable extent (4.46). By the end of the eleventh century, London was easily the most populous place in the kingdom, a position which the city may have reached as early as the tenth century, and which it has maintained ever since.

4.3   Continuous occupation of an exceptional density over a period of two thousand years has given London some of the deepest archaeological deposits in the country (5.3). Although these have been extensively, and in very many places even totally destroyed (figs.6 and 7), areas partially intact still remain scattered throughout the City, and by a remarkable chance the archaeologically vital deposits along the river front are still comparatively undamaged (5.9).

4.4   London's archaeological deposits are not only deep, they are very extensive. The area enclosed by the Roman city wall of c.A.D.200 was approximately 133·5 hectares (330 acres), including the Cripplegate fort of about 4·7 hectares (12 acres). On this basis London was by far the largest of the walled towns of Roman Britain, exceeding its nearest rival, Cirencester, by nearly 40 hectares (14. Rivet 1958, figs.3–5). The size of the walled area can only provide a rough guide, however, reflecting the relative importance of Roman London in its heyday at the end of the second century. A more accurate ranking of the towns of Roman Britain would have to take account of the growth of the occupied area, of the density of occupation within the walls (when these were eventually built), and of the extent of suburban settlement. Our knowledge of Roman, as of early medieval, London is sadly deficient on all these points (4.15 and 35).

4.5   The line of the Roman walls was followed by all subsequent defences of the city down to the seventeenth century. Only on the west, where about 1282 the Blackfriars Priory was extended across the line of the existing wall, was a new line created, increasing the area of the walled city by about 3 hectares (7·5 acres). In common with some other towns of Roman origin such as Winchester or York, it seems likely that the built-up area of late Saxon London exceeded that of the Roman period, not only within the walls, but also in the existence of extensive suburbs outside each of the main gates (4.45). This is, unfortunately, a matter of considerable uncertainty, requiring a great deal of further investigation. It is not therefore until the full medieval period that it is possible to make any reasonably secure general comparison between London and the size of other English medieval walled towns, and then only with the reservations that have already been raised with regard to the Roman period. While such a comparison shows that London did possess the largest walled area, it seems that the disparity between London and its nearest rivals was in this respect not quite so marked as during the Roman period (fig.2). When the intensity of modern redevelopment is recalled (5.13), however, and the depth and extent of London's archaeological deposits are taken into account, the City can be seen to present by far the most extensive problem facing urban archaeology in Britain today.

4.6   It is appropriate, however, that the problem should be seen in a wider context. The great size of modern London among the cities of this planet might lead the casual observer to suppose that this had long been the case, but London, although among the larger Roman towns north of the Alps, was never one of the greatest places of classical antiquity, and even in the middle ages was surpassed in size by several of its nearer neighbours across the Channel (*figs.3a and 3b*). Unlike Paris and Cologne, London was never surrounded by new defences beyond the line of its Roman walls (except for a short period during the Civil War). Unlike Brussels, Bruges, Ghent, or Novgorod, the growth of its population in medieval times was not so great, nor the condition of the country such, that successive lines of defence were required, although this pattern can sometimes be seen in English towns like Northampton or Bristol (*fig.2*).

4.7   The development of London was not constricted in the early modern period, as it was for many of the other European towns illustrated here, by complex lines of bastioned fortification. Nor was its archaeology extensively destroyed by their construction, as at Mainz or Metz. The threat to London's archaeology has come in more recent times through its emergence as an imperial and financial centre of world status, essentially during the reign of Victoria (*5.4*). Our task now is to assess what has been learnt of ancient London through discoveries made and excavations undertaken in the course of repeated rebuilding during the last century, to discern the major problems, and to estimate the extent to which, and the time within which, they can still be solved.

The archaeology of Roman London

4.8   The Roman period has always cast a spell of particular fascination upon those who have laboured to record the archaeology of the City. As a result we are better informed about the archaeology of the four centuries of Roman London than about the archaeology of the succeeding twelve centuries of English rule (*fig.4*). But the comparative intensity of observation relating to the Roman city must be seen in some detail if its true value is to emerge (*Map 2*). There have been comparatively few controlled excavations, some fifty-seven in all, unevenly distributed over the walled area, with a marked concentration in the districts which suffered most from bombing in 1939–45 (cf. *fig.1*). More than a third of these controlled excavations (23 sites) are in the area of the Cripplegate fort; another sixth (11 sites) lie elsewhere along the line of the city wall. More than half the properly conducted excavations have thus been concerned with the defences, with the perimeter areas of the Roman city. Of the remaining excavations two-thirds have lain to the west of Walbrook (14 sites), and one-third to the east (9 sites). Only these nine investigations have taken

place in the area where Roman London began and was most densely developed. This is the situation behind our almost total lack of hard information relating to the origins of the city. It is inevitable that this uneven distribution should have left large areas untouched by modern techniques of excavation, especially in a vast arc to the south, east, and north of Cornhill; along the river frontage; and in the area west and south of St Paul's.

4.9   In general the observations of archaeological deposits made with varying accuracy in the course of construction work conform to the distribution of controlled excavations, with particular concentrations to either side of Gracechurch Street, and along Bush Lane, both areas where the remains of major Roman public buildings have attracted particular attention. While there can be no doubt of the value of these observations in recovering the lines of Roman streets, or elements in the plan of major buildings, they are rarely of great use in providing firm evidence for the date of structures, or in recovering traces of earthworks and timber buildings. Although *Map 2* may thus seem at first sight to suggest that much has been done to record the archaeological evidence for Roman London, it is the distribution of the symbols denoting controlled excavation which gives a fairer picture, with all the limitations discussed in the last paragraph. If it is further recalled that most of these excavations have been single trenches (*3.13*), and that the first area excavations have only recently been undertaken (*3.13, 19*), the many unsolved problems relating to Roman London to be discussed in the following paragraphs will occasion no real surprise.

4.10   Archaeological observation and limited excavation have revealed fragments of the buildings of Roman London, mostly unrelated one to another, but have been less successful in establishing the overall topography of the Roman city (*Map 2*), or in reconstructing the outlines of its historical development. The principal advances have been made in two ways. The study of the distribution of dated finds, principally of samian ware but also including coins, has allowed the area of Claudian occupation to be roughly defined (*3.* Lambert 1915, 269–74; *3.* Pryce and Oswald 1928, 73–110), and the extent of two serious fires to be estimated, one of *c.*A.D.60, probably the result of the revolt of Boudicca, and another of *c.*125–30 (*3.* Dunning 1945; cf. *3.* Merrifield 1965, 90–1). The application of carefully planned and controlled excavation has also had notable successes. The discovery and elucidation of the Cripplegate fort in 1947–65 by Grimes must always rank as one of the triumphs of archaeological method; the establishment of the true character of the Walbrook river and the history of its silting has been of great value; and as a result of repeated

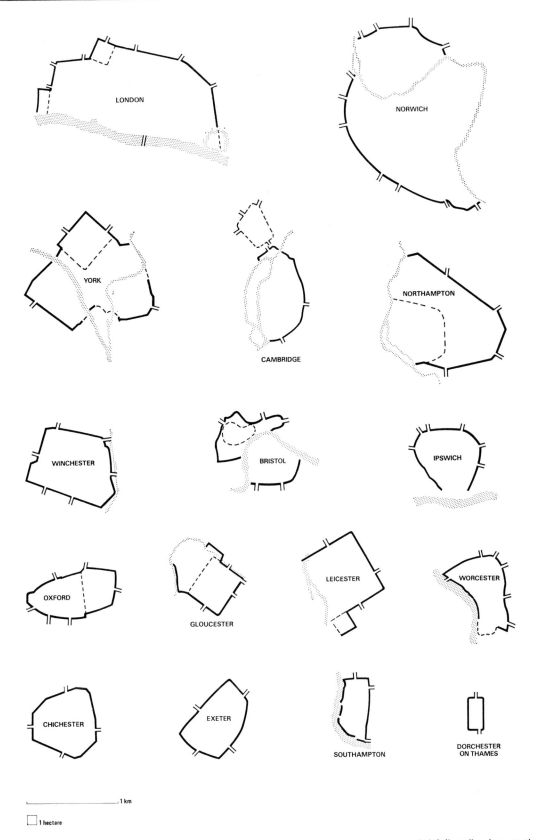

Fig.2 London and some other medieval walled towns in England (1 : 40,000). *The walls are shown at their full medieval extent, the broken lines indicating the course of earlier defences or uncertain stretches of the final circuits*

opportunities carefully taken, our knowledge of the city wall of Roman London and of its date (but *not* the dates of its bastions) is now considerable (*11.* Grimes 1968, 15–40, 47–56, 92–8; *3.* Merrifield 1965, 101–11; *3.* Merrifield 1969, 117–32).

4.11 The historical evolution of the Roman city cannot however be derived from these results alone, and has in fact been little studied. We have only a glimpse of the real complexities of four centuries of crowded and eventful urban life, of a period as long as that which has elapsed since the first Elizabeth addressed her troops at Tilbury. The origins of the city are particularly obscure and can only be reconstructed by analogy with the early history of other Roman towns in Britain. The view usually put forward is based on what may be called the 'military model', a fort with a growing civil *vicus*, replaced by a civilian settlement, providing the genesis of the later town (*3.* Merrifield 1969, 10–27, and for a more decided view *3.* Rodwell 1972). This seems the most likely solution, but the actual evidence for it is almost non-existent, and there may be other possibilities, such as a purely civilian origin, although the course of events in A.D.43 makes this perhaps less probable. The uncertainties surrounding the origin of the Roman settlement serve to indicate the seriousness of the gaps in our knowledge. An outline of the evolution of the town has of course been drawn, and the changing status of Roman London has been usefully discussed by Merrifield (*3.* 1969, 68–84): capital of the province by shortly after A.D.60, London was the seat of the governor, of the financial administration of the procurator, and of the imperial cult. Sometime after A.D.197, when Britain was divided into two provinces, London became the capital of *Britannia Superior*, and at the end of the third century, when Britain was further divided, the city seems to have been the capital of the senior province, *Maxima Caesariensis*, and the seat of the vicar of the secular diocese into which the four British provinces were then grouped. It was thus the centre of the civil administration, and of financial organization, and in the latter part of the fourth century was renamed *Augusta*. In the last official record of the Roman administration, the city was still the seat of the treasury.

4.12 What then are the specific problems requiring solution? Despite very considerable discussion the site of the Roman bridge, or of the successive bridges, for there may have been several, has never been established. This problem should have a high priority, for on its solution depends much of what we may think both of the origins of London, and of the topography of the later Roman city (**69**).⋆ The nature of the earliest occupation north of the bridgehead has never been established, but there are indications of an early planned area on Cornhill which may

suggest the presence of a fort, conceivably a military supply-base, with its attendant *vicus*. There are traces of early cemeteries to the west, south and east of this area, on the slopes above the Walbrook and above the Thames, and in Fenchurch Street. Nothing is known of the stages by which this nucleus became the settlement *cognomento quidem coloniae non insigne, sed copia negotiatorum et commeatuum maxime celebre* described by Tacitus (*Annals* XIV. 33) and destroyed by Boudicca in A.D.60. Our ignorance is not surprising in view of the very few controlled excavations which have taken place here (*4.8*), but the area is already so severely damaged by deep basements (*Map 5*, cf. *fig.7.2*), that every opportunity needs to be taken to carry out investigations in this part of the City (**62, 63, 71, 76, 83, 84, 85, 90, 112, 115**).

4.13 The state of Roman London in the decade following the Boudiccan destruction is not at all clear, but the replanning and extension of the occupied area must have begun around this time for there is ample evidence that London was now the capital of the province (*4.11*). One of the most urgent requirements is further knowledge of the Flavian street plan, which probably extended now to the west of Walbrook. Dating of the evolution of the street plan will come with the location and investigation of further streets, of which at present only the barest outlines are known (*Map 2*). It seems highly probable that London was at this time protected by earthen defences, as it may have been even before Boudicca's attack, but nothing certain is known of their line, or even of their existence. Discoveries here can only come at first by chance, but the problem emphasizes the need to observe all contractor's excavations, and to carry out investigations in advance of site works wherever possible. Considerable attention has recently been devoted to the public buildings constructed in this period, the 'palace' in the Bush Lane area and the baths at Huggin Hill, but others such as the amphitheatre, the theatre, and the temple of the imperial state cult have never been found. The forum with its enormous basilica poses a special problem. Neither its plan nor its structural history are yet properly understood, yet the greater part of its site has now been destroyed or severely damaged (*fig.7.2*). Parts of the site have at last been scheduled under the Ancient Monuments Acts, and it is essential that every development in this area should be preceded by full-scale archaeological excavation (**76, 83, 84**).

4.14 The history of the waterfront is critical for all periods of London's archaeology, and not least for that of the Roman city. Here lie the wharves and

⋆Bold figures in parentheses refer to future developments listed in Appendix I, and shown on *Map 8*, and indicate sites whose investigation may be relevant to the particular problems under discussion.

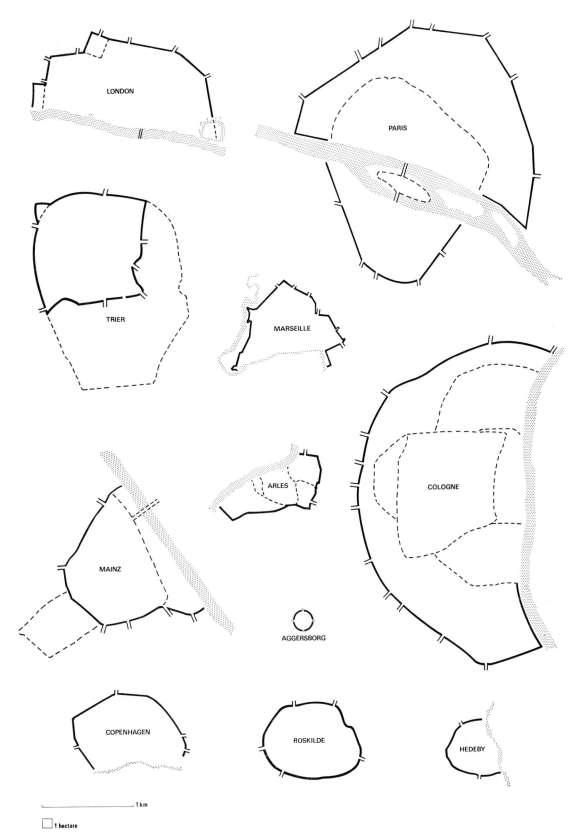

Fig.3a London and some other medieval walled towns in Europe, first series (1:40,000). *The walls are shown at their full medieval extent, the broken lines indicating the course of earlier defences*

jetties of Roman London, the retaining walls of the river, and even the wrecks of Roman ships and their cargoes, such as that found at Blackfriars in 1962 (*3.* Marsden 1967*b*). The depth of the archaeological deposits along the waterfront is considerable (*fig.5*), and they are still remarkably undamaged by comparison with other areas of the city (*figs.6 and 7.3*). Much of the greatest importance about Roman London, its gradual spread along the river, the position of its bridges (*4.12*), and its commercial history can be learnt from investigations in this area between Upper and Lower Thames Street and the Thames. Only one controlled excavation has so far taken place in this entire length (*Map 2*), where large areas are at present under development or shortly to be taken over for this purpose (*fig.7.3, cf. Map 8*). The waterfront thus presents one of the major challenges facing the archaeology of the Roman city (**2, 15, 16, 18, 20, 38, 42, 43, 45, 46, 67, 69, 70, 96**).

4.15   There are so many problems concerning the Roman town of the second, third and fourth centuries that it is only possible to deal with them here in a very general way. The determination of the extent and density of the built-up area at any one time is of particular importance, not only within the walls when built, but also outside the gates. The nature of suburban occupation is at present quite uncertain, and the city may have had only one true suburb, across the river in Southwark. Knowledge of the cemeteries is also very defective. Unfortunately these problems are now to a great extent incapable of solution, and the extent of occupation suggested here (*fig.9.1 and 2*) is frankly hypothetical. It is worth noting, however, that much of the development now imminent concerns the outer areas of the city (*fig.8 and Map 8*), and it seems likely that a great deal of new information regarding the spread of Roman London will become available during the next five years. These regions are of largely unknown archaeological potential, but the discovery of an early Roman fort at Aldgate in 1972, together with complex traces of first-century A.D. timber buildings, shows how rewarding the apparently peripheral areas can be.

4.16   Undoubtedly one of the most difficult problems of fourth-century London is the dating of the bastions added to the city wall. The present situation is not at all satisfactory, for the simple rule that the bastions on the eastern part of the wall are solid and datable to the late Roman period, while those to the west are hollow and of thirteenth-century date (broadly accepted on the maps and figures illustrating this survey) does not always hold and is based on evidence from a quite insufficient number of places, and on really clear evidence only from Bastions 6 and 11a (*Britannia* 3 (1972), 335;

11. Grimes 1968, 64–78, where all the necessary cautions are sounded). Here again there can be few chances left to obtain fresh information, and any that arise will obviously need to be fully grasped.

4.17   Late Roman London was wealthy and well defended, and at the end of the fourth century it was still the seat of the provincial treasury. It has often been pointed out that we know little of this period because the late Roman layers have tended to suffer from medieval disturbance. This is not really an acceptable argument, for it would apply equally to the disturbance of layers of any period by later activity, and recent work has at last begun to show that late and even sub-Roman deposits do exist. Objects datable to the fifth century are rarely found and until recently the most striking have been the pewter ingots stamped with the name of Syagrius, found up-river at Battersea, and the Tower hoard which although strictly of the very late fourth century must surely have been deposited in the fifth (*3.* Merrifield 1969, 201; *14.* Painter 1972, 87; the attribution of the ingots to the fifth-century ruler of Gaul has been questioned by J. P. C. Kent). Now, however, imported sherds of mediterranean amphorae of fifth or sixth-century date ('B' ware) have been found at St Katherine Coleman (Fenchurch Street), St. Dionis Backchurch (Lime Street), in Bush Lane, and in the Coal Exchange bath-house, Billingsgate (*4.* Cook 1969*b*), and the latter site has also produced from the debris of its destruction an Anglo-Saxon applied saucer brooch of the same general date (*4.* Cook 1969*a*). It is probably no coincidence that some of these finds have come from immediately behind the waterfront, for parts of this area would probably have continued in occupation even when much of the Roman town was in decay. The pewter ingots and the B-ware sherds both suggest long-distance trade connections. London is the only town of eastern Britain where such amphorae have been found and identified, their distribution normally reflecting the continued use of the Atlantic routes between western Britain and the mediterranean. Excavations in this area may thus be expected to produce further evidence for late and sub-Roman London (**68, 92–5, 101, 102**), while the evidence of the riverfront deposits may be of critical importance (*4.14*).

4.18   Other aspects of sub-Roman London which deserve study include the survival of fragments of the Roman street plan into later periods (*4.36*), and the question of suburban churches (*4.29*). The evidence for the existence of Roman suburban buildings below extra-mural churches such as St Bride, Fleet Street (*11.* Grimes 1968, 182–4), and St Andrew, Holborn (*3.* Merrifield 1969, 137), to mention only those closest to the walls, is striking. While stressing that there is at present no evidence

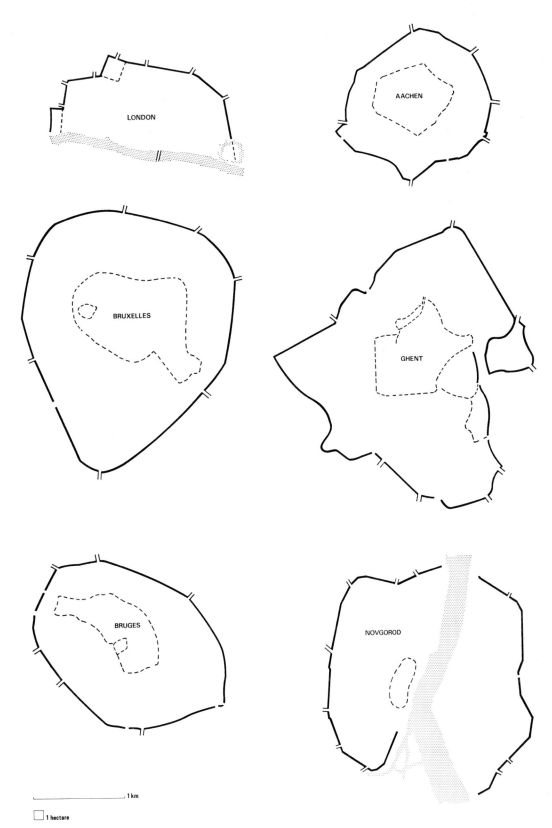

Fig.3b London and some other medieval walled towns in Europe, second series (1 : 40,000). *The walls are shown at their full medieval extent, the broken lines indicating the course of earlier defences*

for continuity in the use of these sites, it is important to recognize the part which extra-mural cemeteries and churches are now playing in study of the evolution of other northern towns from the Roman into the medieval period (e.g. Mainz, *14*. Weidemann 1968; and Metz, *14*. Weidemann 1970). With increasing evidence for continuity of occupation within the walls, the interest of the suburban cemeteries and their structures becomes of increasing importance for the history of late and sub-Roman London (**1–14, 21–3, 25–35, 54, 61, 81, 82, 103–6, 111, 118, 121–5, 127–8, 130–1**). There is no evidence that the intra-mural churches of later periods are likely to have been established on sites of Romano-British Christianity.

4.19   This brief survey of some of the problems facing the archaeology of Roman London suggests that two areas are of very special importance, the Thames frontage, and the nucleus of the early city occupying the hill top, Cornhill, and the river slopes to the west and south. Of the major problems requiring urgent attention, the site of the bridge, the growth and character of the early nucleus on Cornhill, the evolution and pattern of the street system, and the varying extent of occupation, together with the cemeteries of all periods, are among the most important. Even where proper archaeological excavations cannot be undertaken, it seems essential that every disturbance of the ground should be watched to recover traces of buildings and particularly finds of pottery and coins which can be used to plot the changing boundaries of occupation throughout the Roman period. What was achieved half a century ago for the earliest phases of the Roman city (*4.10*) should surely now be applied to the stages of its later evolution.

The archaeology of Anglo-Saxon London

4.20   The archaeology of Anglo-Saxon London barely exists as an organized field of inquiry. Chance discovery and observation, which has contributed so much to our knowledge of the Roman city, has made little impact on the study of its successor. This is partly because Anglo-Saxon buildings were usually of timber rather than stone (and it will be remembered that observation of builders' excavations has by and large failed to reveal Roman timber buildings or earthworks:*4·9*), but it is also the result of a tendency to concentrate upon the study of Roman London without an equal regard for the archaeology of the city's subsequent periods (*fig.4*). It may certainly be argued that this neglect arises partly from the comparatively recent growth of interest in Anglo-Saxon and later medieval archaeology, but this does not lessen the unbalance of the present situation. Since observation of building sites has yielded so little of interest regarding the Anglo-Saxon city, apart from the few chance finds of objects shown on

Map 3, it is only from controlled excavations that information has been recovered regarding the buildings of this period, let alone the development of Anglo-Saxon city as a whole. There have been eleven such excavations, widely distributed over the City and its immediate area. The coverage is so inadequate (*fig.4*) that there is little to be gained by pointing to omissions. But nothing underlines the lack of thought given to Anglo-Saxon London more than the total failure to investigate the river frontage, the one area where the usual view – that the Anglo-Saxon and medieval layers have already been destroyed by modern cellars – is known not to apply.

4.21   The most useful results have been achieved by the excavation of churches. Notable among these are the investigations of St Bride, Fleet Street, and St Alban, Wood Street (*11*. Grimes 1968, 182–97, 203–9). Other excavations have been limited in scope and only one has produced more than the slightest traces of domestic occupation, when sunken-floored huts were found in 1955 on the Financial Times site in Cannon Street (*11*. Grimes 1968, 155–60).

4.22   In this situation it is virtually impossible to draw any valid conclusions regarding Anglo-Saxon London based on the archaeological evidence alone. Sir Mortimer Wheeler's two catalogues, together with their introductions, *London and the Saxons*, published in 1935, and *London and the Vikings* which appeared in 1927, still remain the only surveys of the archaeology of the six centuries between the breakdown of Romano-British urban life and the Norman Conquest. Although the former has been in part superseded in its account of London and its region in the fifth and sixth centuries, the two books are in other particulars unreplaced.

4.23   Since the archaeological evidence for Anglo-Saxon London is at present so limited, the development of the city during this period can be followed only by fitting the available historical and archaeological facts into the general pattern of early medieval urban evolution as it is currently understood in England and on the continent. This pattern has changed out of all recognition in the last forty years. Such an approach may lead to some conclusions about the size and character of Anglo-Saxon London at various stages in its history. And these conclusions may in turn help to define the archaeological problems, and suggest ways in which they may be solved and fresh information obtained. Whatever advances are to be made in the future, it is at least abundantly clear that these must be based on a combination of the available lines of inquiry, historical, archaeological, and topographical, together with more specialist fields such as numismatics, place-name, and legal studies. As already

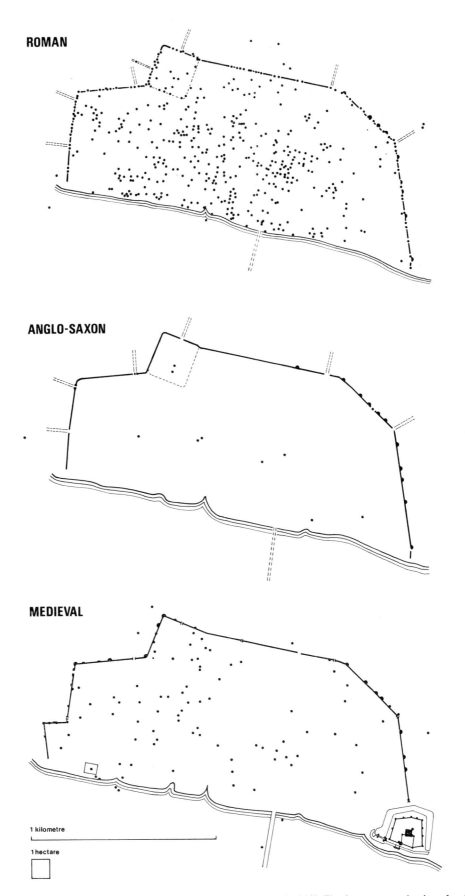

ROMAN

ANGLO-SAXON

MEDIEVAL

1 kilometre

1 hectare

Fig.4 Archaeology in the City : the emphasis of research (1 :20,000). *The dots represent the sites of archaeological excavations and observations as shown on Maps 2–4*

indicated, this whole pattern will then need to be controlled and interpreted within a framework of comparative information about the origins and growth of early medieval towns elsewhere in Europe. It is perhaps this last consideration which has so far received least attention. It may also offer some of the most profitable lines of inquiry.

London A.D.400–600

4.24   There is ample evidence for the existence of a flourishing community (in contemporary terms) at London from A.D.600 onwards. To this we shall come in due course (*4.30*). Meanwhile our first purpose must be to see what evidence there is for continued occupation in the two centuries after about A.D.400. Something has already been said, from the Roman side as it were, of the wealth and status of London at the end of the fourth and in the earlier fifth century (*4.11, 17,* and *18*). Archaeological evidence of the kind already available from Verulamium (St Albans), for the continuance of Romano-British town-life until the middle of the fifth century, and written evidence for conditions at the time of St Germanus' visits to Britain in 429 and 447, make it clear enough that London would have been unusual in south-eastern Britain if it were not still in some sense an organized community as late as A.D.440–50 (*14.* Frere 1967, 357–83). It was to London that the British retreated after their defeat by the English at *Creacanford* in 456–7. And for one writer of about A.D.480 Britain was still a very rich island. This is the context of the Syagrius ingots and the amphorae of mediterranean fabric from London (*4.17*). But although the existence of a fifth-century London need not be doubted, archaeological evidence of its presence is still very thin. The view that the material culture of this period was archaeologically 'negative', in the sense that it comprised little that would physically have survived the centuries (*4.* Wheeler 1935, 41–2), can no longer be maintained (*14.* Alcock 1971, 197–252). The small quantity of the finds of this period reflects rather the chances of discovery, for it is not to be supposed that more than limited areas of the walled city were still occupied. Archaeology seems as yet not to have lighted upon them, although the discoveries at Billingsgate and Bush Lane may suggest the importance of areas near to the river (*4.17*).

4.25   The greatest change in our picture of late Roman London since 1935 must be the recognition of the presence of Germanic people in and around the city as early as the latter part of the fourth century. The identification of late Roman military equipment and its discovery in London suggests the presence of an alien and probably Germanic garrison required to maintain and man the artillery mounted on the bastions of the city wall (*14.* Hawkes and Dunning 1961, 15–21; *14.* Frere 1966). In

several towns of Roman Britain, including London, this metalwork is complemented by Romano-British pottery in a style that seems to be influenced by Germanic taste (*14.* Myres 1969, 66–70). Anglo-Saxon pottery of a very early date has itself now been found in or immediately outside a number of Roman walled towns (*14.* Myres 1969, 62–83), and the evidence is increasing (*14.* Biddle 1972, 101–2; *14.* Cunliffe 1970, 68–70). This latter pottery has not yet been identified in London, but it is known from a series of sites in the Thames valley and estuary, its distribution coinciding with that of the metalwork just discussed, which has itself been found in the City. There is thus increasing evidence for Anglo-Saxon groups 'officially settled on the main route into the heart of Roman Britain by the very early years of the fifth century' (*14.* Myres 1969, 78, cf. *14.* Jones 1968, 222–8). The population of late and sub-Roman London and its immediate region was therefore mixed, with a substantial Germanic element.

4.26   It remains true, nevertheless, that there is a marked absence of Anglo-Saxon cemeteries of the mid to later fifth and sixth centuries in the immediate area of London (*4.* Wheeler 1935, 54–5). This led Wheeler to the view that Anglo-Saxon settlers avoided the area, that they were in fact kept out by the relatively dense and well-organized sub-Roman population. Such settlement as there was took place peacefully, and the settlers soon merged with the existing population. An extension of this view produced the so-called 'sub-Roman triangle', an area lying to both sides of the Thames and including Colchester and Verulamium as well as London, Rochester, and Canterbury (*4.* Wheeler 1935, 58–9, fig.2). 'The triangle' has not found much favour and can now be seen to have been a considerable over-simplification. But the basic idea, that there may be areas of Roman Britain where the new Anglo-Saxon settlers tended to be absorbed by the existing population, only later asserting their own dominant identity, deserves closer attention. The new evidence for early fifth-century Anglo-Saxon settlement in towns whose vicinity is notably avoided by pagan Saxon cemeteries until a century later (Canterbury and Winchester are the obvious cases; Portchester is analogous) suggests just such a process. A comparable development is seen also on the upper Rhine in Switzerland, an area conquered by the Alamanni in the late fifth century. Here the population of the Roman walled forts and towns survived, and continued to use their own cemeteries, only gradually during the sixth century becoming influenced by Alamannic customs. Meanwhile in the surrounding countryside the Alamanni set up their own villages and established new cemeteries. Outside the walled places, there was no continuity from the Roman period (*14.* Böhner 1966, 307–12).

4.27 The absence of Anglo-Saxon cemeteries from the area around London is not therefore necessarily evidence that the Anglo-Saxons avoided this area, but that within it their settlement was limited and their culture absorbed. This alone implies the survival in London of a dominant element, a controlling presence in the walled city which is the only conceivable focus of the area. The survival of walled towns under the control of their own inhabitants seems to have been assured for a considerable period in areas of other than overwhelming conquest or treaty settlement by the very strength of their walls and the arrangements made to defend them (*14.* Frere 1966; *14.* Böhner 1966). That a town also controlled a territory around it is sufficiently obvious, and in some sense this territory must be defined around London by the area from which Anglo-Saxon cemeteries are absent. There are however, several different territories. There is the *pomerium* of the Roman city reaching out perhaps one-and-a-half to two-and-a-half miles from the city gates (*3.* Rodwell 1972, 43–53, cf. remarks by A. L. F. Rivet, *Britannia 1* (1970), 38–9); there is the larger area of perhaps five-miles radius avoided by Anglo-Saxon cemeteries (*4.* Wheeler 1935, 54–5); and there is the vast area stretching into Middlesex, Hertfordshire, Kent, and Surrey over which, perhaps as early as the Anglo-Saxon period, the citizens of London had rights of hunting (*4.* Wheeler 1935, 59–62). These various territories need further study, particularly in the light of evidence relating to the origins of *oppidum* and *banlieu* now available from the continent (*14.* Lombard-Jourdan 1972), and certainly applicable to this country (*14.* Biddle, 1974). It is a field where a fresh examination of the written evidence for the early history of boundaries in the London area may have much to tell us.

4.28 It is possible to conclude, as did Wheeler in 1935, although for rather different reasons, that there was 'a continuing, if unexalted, civic consciousness in London throughout the 5th and 6th centuries' (*4.* 1935, 83). Compared to the Roman city, the London of this period must have been impoverished, but whether it was relatively poor in the circumstances of its time may be doubted. The mediterranean amphorae and the ingots already mentioned (*4.17*) are a fairly sure sign that it was not. It seems in any case to have been sufficiently powerful to control the settlement of its immediate hinterland, although during the course of the later fifth or sixth centuries it was either conquered by the English, or (and this is perhaps more likely) passed peacefully under their control after a long period of cultural assimilation.

4.29 It is scarcely possible to plan the archaeological investigation of so evanescent a period of London's past. Much will depend on chance finds, a conclusion which underlines yet again the vital need to observe for archaeological purposes all disturbances of the soil within the City's limits. It may also be possible to follow existing clues. The most promising of these is the hint from Billingsgate of the importance of the waterfront (*4.17*), an area where further sites are soon to be redeveloped (**66–69, 92–96, 101–102**). The economic basis of fifth and sixth-century London, restricted as it may have been by comparison with other periods, must have relied relatively as much on water-borne traffic. The mediterranean amphorae are a sign of this (*14.* Alcock 1971, 208, map), and further evidence may be recovered from anywhere along the City's frontage on the Thames. There is, finally, the question of Christianity. The problems of the extra-mural churches and cemeteries have already been mentioned (*4.18*). The framework suggested here for the cultural evolution of London between A.D.400 and A.D.600 (*4.27*) carries with it the possibility that the Christian tradition was uninterrupted in London, or at least interrupted for a much shorter period than has so far been imagined. It is commonly accepted that Christianity continued unbroken in the Rhineland, although the latest thinking would see a gap of perhaps a generation on many sites. At St Albans there is no reason to postulate a much longer interval (*14.* Morris 1968 provides some of the evidence), perhaps in the later sixth century. The same may be true of London, and the possibility should not be ignored. The suburban churches, founded within the cemeteries of the Roman city, are those most likely to be relevant in this context (the abbey at St Albans is suburban in relation to the Roman city). Their occurrence on the sites of Roman suburban buildings certainly requires more thought (*4.18*), and every opportunity should be taken to carry out further investigations wherever an existing church is altered or the site of a former church, or the area surrounding it, developed.

London A.D.600–800

4.30 By the year 601 London, or the tradition of its former greatness, was still sufficiently substantial for Pope Gregory to designate the city as the primary see of England. The course of events in Kent decreed a different future, and in 604 Augustine appointed Mellitus to be bishop of the East Saxons with his see in London. With the reversion of the East Saxons to paganism about 616, Mellitus was excluded from London, and it was not until 653–4 that the episcopal succession was re-established. It was never again interrupted.

4.31 In the early seventh century London and the East Saxon province were subject to Kent, whose supremacy was seen in 604 when Ethelbert of Kent built the church of St Paul in London for the episcopal see. The evidence for the existence of a royal residence in the city is fairly clear. Sixteenth-century tradition placed the palace of Ethelbert in Aldermanbury to the north-east of St Paul's, while in the thirteenth century Matthew Paris believed that the adjacent church of St Alban, Wood Street, had been a chapel of Offa of Mercia, and contiguous with his palace (*Map 3*, cf. *4*. Wheeler 1935, 103–4). Excavation has revealed the Anglo-Saxon church of St Alban and the existence of late Saxon occupation on the traditional site of the palace (*11*. Grimes 1968, 159, 203–9). Proof of the existence of a Kentish royal residence of the seventh century is provided, however, by the Laws of Hlothhere and Eadric of 673–85 (?), where the king's hall in London is specifically mentioned (*4*. Whitelock 1955, 631). The apparent location of the royal residence within the limits of the Roman Cripplegate fort, and more specifically within its south-east quarter, is of considerable interest, for the medieval and modern streets in this area seem to preserve a memory of the principal streets of the fort, and may thus imply that the fort itself survived as a distinct, and possibly still defensible, enclosure into the Saxon period (*11*. Grimes 1968, 29, 39, 204 *note*). The blocking of the west gate of the fort (*ibid*. 32) may therefore reflect the continuing defence of this enclosure, rather than the shutting of an entry into the walled city as a whole. Of the later history of the royal residence and the *burh* within which it stood, there is little evidence. By the eleventh century royal interest had shifted to Westminster, and the former royal precinct in the city had in some way become *ealdormannes burh,* the fortified enclosure of the alderman, the modern Aldermanbury (*2*. Page 1923, 140, 142; *5*. Stenton 1960, 188–9; *7*. Ekwall 1954, 13, 195). The possibility that this enclosure may have been formed by the still surviving defences of the Roman fort, and may indeed at an early stage have been identical with it, opens a new and so far unexplored inquiry.

4.32   The location of the folkmoot, the 'first in dignity, as doubtless it was first in age' of London's institutions (*5*. Stenton 1960, 186), between St Paul's and the traditional site of the royal residence, is particularly relevant in an attempt to establish the functions and physical components of the Anglo-Saxon city. The period of origin of the London folkmoot is unknown, but is probably anterior to the reign of Alfred. The discovery of an early seventh-century assembly-place in the form of a *cuneus* of a Roman theatre at the Northumbrian royal palace of Yeavering (*5*. Colvin 1963, 2–4) should serve as a reminder not only of the potentially early date of the London folkmoot, and of its relatively close spatial association with both the palace and the bishop's see, but also of its possible physical character. In London, as in Northumbria, there must still in the seventh century have been visible the ruins of the assembly-places, the theatre and amphitheatre, of an earlier age.

4.33   The early importance of London is emphasized by its coins, for it was the only place before the 820s to issue a major coinage under its own name. Gold tremisses or *thrymsas* with the legend LONDVNIV appeared about 640 and were followed in the next century, possibly as late as *c.*730, by the 'London inscribed' silver sceattas bearing the legend LVNDONIA. The latter must have formed a relatively large issue or issues for they gave rise to the 'London derived' and 'London connected' series, as well as a number of copies. None of these derivative types need necessarily be from a London mint, and some were certainly imitated in Frisia. London's part in the minting of the penny, first struck in Kent towards the end of the third quarter of the eighth century, is obscure until the reign of Egbert of Wessex, who issued coins with the legend LVNDONIA CIVIT[AS] about 829. Offa and later Mercian kings may have struck coins in London, but without the evidence of a mint-signature, the picture must remain uncertain. According to current numismatic opinion, however, London had replaced Canterbury as the main English mint by the latter part of the ninth century and perhaps by as early as *c.*865.

4.34   The law code of Hlothhere and Eadric of 673–85(?) is partly concerned with Kentish men trading in London. Transactions were regulated by the king's reeve (*wīc–gerēfa*), and the place itself was *Lundenwic*. The meaning of *wīc* in this context is probably 'town' or 'market town', and is comparable to *Hamwih* (Southampton), *Sondwic* (Sandwich), *Gipeswic* (Ipswich), or *Eoforwicceaster* (York), all places for which there is evidence of extensive trading and/or industrial activity in the seventh and following centuries. For Bede, writing in the 720s, London was the metropolis of the East Saxons, 'a mart of many peoples coming by land and sea' (*multorum emporium populorum terra marique uenientium: H. E.* ii. 3). During the eighth and ninth centuries Mercian and Kentish kings served incidentally to record the importance of London's sea-borne trade by granting to bishops or the heads of monastic houses the right to send ships into the port of London, free of dues exacted by the tax-gatherers, *nedbaderas* (*2*. Page 1923, 34–5; *14*. Robertson 1939, no.1 and cf. 259–60). In 811, in connection with a meeting of the council, London was described as a famous place and a royal town (*in loco praeclaro oppidoque regali Lundaniae vicu: BCS* 335). Although the overlordship of London was on occasion briefly in the hands of Wessex, for example at the turn of the seventh and eighth centuries, and from 752 for about twenty years, the city was for one and a half centuries normally under Mercian control. During this period

London seems to have been the principal trading-town of the Mercian kingdom, probable route, for example, of the contacts between Offa and Charlemagne. The city thus served Mercia, as *Hamwih* (Southampton) served Wessex, or York did Northumbria. The overlordship of Egbert of Wessex after 825, and the Danish attacks and capture of London in the following decades, marked fifty years of change, which were only brought to an end by Alfred's restoration of the city in 886 onwards.

4.35   This survey of London's major functional components in the seventh to ninth centuries may enable us to make some approach to the problem of the city's size during this period. Most striking is the combination of royal and ecclesiastical functions on the one hand, with economic functions (and especially trade) on the other, for in the case of Wessex these functions seem to have been divided at this period between Winchester and Southampton respectively. Even so Anglo-Saxon Hamwih occupied an area of some 30 hectares. It seems most unlikely that contemporary London was smaller. But it is equally clear that London, with a total walled area of 133·5 hectares, never began to approach the size of Dorestad, which may have attained an area of over 240 hectares. In seeking to come to grips with the problem of London's archaeology in the seventh to ninth centuries we shall probably not be far wrong, therefore, in thinking that between one quarter and one half of the Roman walled area may have been occupied (*fig.9.3*).

4.36   The relative sparseness of archaeological material from this period of London's history is quite inconsistent with the picture which can thus be derived from a combination of historical and comparative archaeological evidence. It may be worthwhile therefore to call attention to some specific problems which require solution, and which may in turn throw some light on this period. The evolution of London's street plan in the early middle ages has never received the attention it deserves. In some places elements of the Roman street pattern seem to have survived with little change, as in the Cripplegate fort (*4.31*). Elsewhere lengths of the two most important east-west streets of the Roman town have remained in use, while along intervening stretches of the same streets, the medieval and modern courses have wandered away from the earlier lines. Examples of such 'wandering streets' can be seen by comparing the lines of Newgate Street, part of Cheapside, the east end of Lombard Street, Fenchurch Street, Aldgate and Aldgate High Street, or of Fleet Street, Watling Street, the east end of Cannon Street and Eastcheap (*Map 1*), with the corresponding Roman streets (*Map 2*). It is striking that in each case the markets – Cheapside (Westcheap) and Eastcheap – occupy approximately the Roman lines. By contrast

the great junction east of the Mansion House has no forerunner in the Roman period. The gathering together at this point of the streets that sweep across the eastern part of the Roman town with scant regard for its former layout suggests that new patterns of settlement conditioned the growth of the new streets at an early period, involving the development of Westcheap and a crossing of the Walbrook valley to the east. Every opportunity needs to be taken to examine such archaeological evidence as may survive for the date of origin of these and any other of London's medieval and modern streets (*10c.* Haslam 1972).

4.37   The existence of the two markets of Westcheap and Eastcheap reflects the physical division of the walled area of the city by the Walbrook. Much has been made of the contrast between the Roman concentration on the east side of Walbrook, and the Anglo-Saxon emphasis on the western bank; between the Roman forum on Cornhill, and the St Paul's area on Ludgate Hill (e.g. *4.* Wheeler 1935, 98–113). That there is a contrast is clear enough, but how it should be interpreted is quite uncertain. Attention has been drawn to the name 'Walbrook', OE *Weala brōc*, 'brook of the Welsh [i.e. Britons] or of the serfs', as if in early Anglo-Saxon London there might have been two ethnic areas, the surviving British to the east, the newly dominant Anglo-Saxon to the west. Too much is here surmise. What is badly needed is fresh information on, for example, the dating of the post-Roman changes in street pattern and the emergence of the western and eastern markets (**58, 71, 90**). Part of the evidence for the supposed contrast comes from the presumed dates of foundation of city churches (*4.* Wheeler 1935, 99–102, fig.4), evidence no longer so clear since the emergence of the early date of All Hallows, Barking (*10e.* Kendrick and Radford 1943; *14.* Taylor and Taylor 1965, 399–400). Further evidence has been claimed from the distribution of finds of the relevant dates, but here too the picture has been changed by new discoveries (e.g., *4.* Cook 1969a), and was in any case based on a very small sample, as would still be the case. The need for the investigation of the sites of city churches as a contribution to the settlement history of London cannot be overstated.

4.38   The known sites of churches and a few other places apart (e.g. the 'Cripplegate' palace and the folkmoot, cf. *4.31* and *4.32*), the location of sites and areas occupied in the seventh to ninth centuries must always remain a matter of chance and the survival of the evidence unaffected by subsequent constructions. The indications of the importance of London as a port during this period (*4.34*) must, however, point yet again (cf. *4.14*) to the archaeology of the waterfront (*fig.9.3*). The process by which the shore has advanced more than 100 m. out into the river from the Roman waterfront is only now beginning to be studied. That the change had begun in the Roman period seems likely, and that it continued throughout the Anglo-Saxon period is probable. Here, if anywhere, the archaeological deposits are still sufficiently intact to provide the history of London's commercial activity during the middle Anglo-Saxon period (**18, 20, 38, 42, 43, 45, 46, 67, 69, 70, 96**). Investigation of the waterfront may also bear on the nature of the river crossing, on the date of abandonment of the Roman bridge, and on the construction of its earliest successors (**68, 69**). As for the defences of the city in this period, or rather the maintenance of the Roman walls, nothing certain is known. All the principal Roman gates were still in use, or at least their sites, but this need not reflect more than the passage of the streets through convenient gaps in the walls. This alone would suggest the continuing importance of the Roman defences as a barrier, but only the fortunate – and unlikely – discovery of contemporary structures at the gates, or added to the walls, will be able to replace speculation on this matter.

London A.D.800–1066

4.39   The formal history of London during the last two centuries of Anglo-Saxon rule is well known and need only be summarized here in the briefest outline. Danish attacks on London began in 842, and the city was stormed in 851. Despite a West Saxon success in the same year, the Vikings seem to have controlled the lower Thames for the next thirty years, until Alfred recovered London by force in 886, and held it during the renewed attacks of 893–5. For almost exactly a century the city enjoyed peace. From 982 onwards, in 994, and repeatedly after 1009 the city was again attacked in the intensified Danish incursions which resulted in the submission of England in 1013. In these years London emerged 'as the dominant factor of the situation. Alone of English cities she now consistently withstood attack' (*4.* Wheeler 1927, 13). There was no doubt of the importance of London's defiance: 'Praise be to God', wrote the chronicler in 1009, 'it stands still untouched, and they always suffered loss there'. But in 1013, after resisting in full battle, and following the collapse of opposition in the rest of the country, London at last submitted. Following Swein's death in February 1014, the city was again independent of Danish control, and although once more besieged in 1016, she remained unconquered until her final submission towards the end of the year. When all England paid tribute in 1018, London paid 10,500 pounds, one-eighth of the total for the country. For the next fifty years the city was again at peace, submitting to William in November 1066, after a short siege (*5.* Morton and Muntz 1972, xlix–liv).

4.40   The long-sustained and successful defence of London against the Danish attacks of the late tenth and early eleventh centuries implies that the physical defences of the city were in good order. That these were based essentially on the Roman city wall of the early third century there can be no doubt. Traces are seen from time to time of repairs which can be broadly dated to the early middle ages (*3.* Merrifield 1969, 125), yet a detailed survey of all that is known of the post-Roman history and structural evolution of the city wall has never been undertaken (but cf. *11.* Grimes 1968, 78–70). It is badly needed. Evidence is also accumulating for an early medieval ditch or recutting of earlier ditches outside the wall (e.g. *11.* Marsden 1969, 20–6; *11.* Marsden 1970, 6–8). The city gates were certainly in use at the beginning of the eleventh century (*Map 3*), but whether the structures were then rebuildings, or simply the Roman gates repaired or maintained from an earlier age, we have little or no means of knowing. Post-Roman but pre-thirteenth century additions and alterations to the gates have been noted on occasion (e.g. *11.* Marsden 1969, 24), but the evidence is very defective. Suffice it to say that the evidence from other late Saxon towns now points to the probability that London was entered by stone gates and surrounded by a multiple ditch system during the last centuries of Saxon rule (*14.* Radford 1970; cf. *14.* Biddle 1974, pt. IV. 2.vi). In 1066 the city was

> *A leua muris, a dextris flumine tuta,*
> *Hostes nec metuit nec pauet arte capi,*

'protected on the left side by the walls, on the right side by the river, it neither fears enemies nor dreads being taken by storm' (*5.* Morton and Muntz 1972, 40–1, lines 639–40). But the wall was not a simple structure, for William threatened not only to destroy it, but to 'raze the bastions to the ground, and bring down the proud tower in rubble',

> *Męnia dissoluet, turres equabit harenis*
> *Elatam turrem destruet aggerie,*

a phrase which is not only of great interest for the history of the bastions (*4.16*), but which also provides a glimpse of a stone tower or particularly massive gate which is otherwise quite unknown (*5.* Morton and Muntz 1972, 42–3, lines 677–8, *note 5*).

4.41   The reconstruction of the Roman defences was the work of Alfred from 886 onwards. After the recovery of the city from the Danes that year Alfred 'refurbished the walls, repopulated the city, and during a conference to discuss its restoration (*instauracio*), assigned to various magnates plots of land bounded by streets' (*4.* Biddle and Hill 1971, 83). Some elements of the London street pattern were already in being by this time (*4.36*), but it seems likely that the subdivision of the larger unoccupied areas between the lines of the main older streets was now begun, forming the rather regular rectilinear plan that is so marked a feature of the area between Upper Thames Street and Gresham Street to the west, and between Lower Thames Street and Fenchurch Street to the east (*fig.9.4*, *Map 4*). Unfortunately there is no direct archaeological or historical evidence for the date of origin of these streets, the few north-south elements on *fig.9.4* usually appearing because their existence at an early date is suggested by the probable date of churches situated along them. The street pattern of medieval London was essentially complete by the twelfth century, but the study of its evolution up to this date has scarcely been begun. If it seems possible to suggest that it was the product of an Alfredian initiative working within the framework of an older system, itself partly of Roman origin, then the evidence is still mostly to seek.

4.42   Two elements, however, can perhaps be reasonably dated. The first is the line Fish Street Hill, Gracechurch Street, Bishopsgate. This route ignores the Roman pattern, but is clearly related to a river-crossing in the approximate position of Old London Bridge (with some flexibility for a site slightly to the east or west). The earliest written evidence for a post-Roman bridge at London dates from between 963 and 984 (*10d.* Honeybourne 1969). It seems possible to argue, however, that the bridge should be as old as the *burh* of Southwark, which was in existence by 919 (*14.* Brooks 1964, 74–5; *14.* Hill 1969). The *burh* was perhaps designed to act as a fortified bridge-head, which with a defended bridge could bar the ascent of the river to hostile ships (*14.* Hill 1970). If this view is correct, the street leading towards the bridge should probably be dated to the late ninth century, the most likely moment for the foundation of Southwark and the reconstruction of the bridge following Alfred's reconquest of London in 886.

4.43   The second potentially datable element in the street pattern of London is the street running within the walls (*Map 4*). This street has no Roman predecessor, except perhaps in the area of the Cripplegate fort, where the *intervallum* road of the fort may have given rise to the northern end of Noble Street and the western end of London Wall (*11.* Grimes 1968, fig.4). In both cases, however, the superimposition may be coincidence, resulting from the construction of the intra-mural street of the city to serve precisely the same purpose as the *intervallum* road of the fort, namely, direct access to the walls in time of war, with the advantage of rapid movement on interior lines. The intra-mural street was once probably continuous around the inside of the city wall (*fig.9.4*), but parts of it have now disappeared, particularly on the west. It is just here, however, that archaeological evidence

for its former existence seems to be available. In a section of the defences on the site of the extension of the Central Criminal Court adjacent to Warwick Square (*11.* Marsden 1970, 4, fig.3, below layer 14), a roadway was found running parallel to the defences. This road, which overlay the Roman bank and fourth-century deposits, was itself overlain by a layer containing an eleventh- or twelfth-century sherd, and was in turn sealed by the medieval bank of the twelfth or thirteenth century. Intra-mural streets are now known to be a characteristic feature of late Saxon town plans (*4.* Biddle and Hill 1971, 76*), and it seems likely that the London intra-mural street should be regarded as part of Alfred's restoration of the city in and after 886.

4.44   Definition of the occupied area of late Saxon London is dependent partly on the dating of the development of the street plan, partly on knowledge of the dates of foundation of the city churches, and partly on study of the distribution of datable finds. Further work is badly needed on all these aspects. Some indication of the extensive spread of churches within the walls at this period is given by *Map 3* and *fig.9.4*. By the thirteenth century there were at least 100 churches within the walls, and city parishes will therefore have occupied on average an area of no more than $3\frac{1}{2}$ acres. If, as Professor Brooke has argued (*2.* Brooke 1968, 17–22; cf. *10e.* Brooke 1970), these churches were essentially, or largely, neighbourhood churches, it may well follow that the origins of a majority of them are to be referred to an early period. Here archaeological evidence may be decisive, and this consideration alone demands the investigation of every church site, or area adjacent to a church, that may be affected by modern development (**36, 44, 48, 49, 54, 58, 60, 69, 73, 74, 76, 77, 80, 99, 107**). The constant observation of all building sites for the collection of datable finds from which distribution maps of the extent of the occupied area at different periods may be compiled is an essential prerequisite for the study of late Saxon London, as it is for other periods (e.g. *4.19*). Only by these methods will it be possible to establish the real size of the occupied area and thus place the essential comparative studies on a sounder basis than that of the crude outline of the defended area which is all that is at present possible (*fig2.*).

4.45   These considerations apply equally to the

---

*Their significance was not fully appreciated when this article was written in 1970. The intra-mural street at Winchester has now been shown by excavation to be an integral feature of the late ninth-century street plan of that city, an observation that probably allows the intra-mural streets of the other Wessex *burhs* to be referred to the same period: *Antiq. J.*, Winchester: tenth interim report, forthcoming.

suburbs. The existence from the pre-conquest period of a number of extra-mural churches points to the development of at least three suburbs, other than Southwark, at an early period (*fig.9.4*). In this respect late Saxon London provides a contrast with the Roman city, for which evidence of suburban development is notably lacking (*4.15*). The situation at London is thus comparable to that of other late Saxon towns of Roman origin, such as Winchester or York, where the extent of suburban development exceeds that of the Roman period. These problems of the extent of the intra-mural occupied area, and of suburban origins and development, are critical for any comparison between the urbanism of Roman Britain and Anglo-Saxon England, as indeed for any comparative study of early medieval towns.

4.46   Whatever difficulties there may be in reaching any accurate understanding of the absolute extent of late Saxon London, there can be no doubt of the relative importance of the city among the towns of contemporary England. The tribute paid by London in 1018 amounted to one-eighth of the amount contributed by the whole country (*4.39*), while an estimate (highly debatable) of London's population in 1086 would make the city between two and three times the size of its nearest rival (*14.* Russell 1948, 284–8). More precise perhaps are the figures now available for the output of the London mint and the number of its moneyers. Of the surviving coins of the period 959–1066, 24% were minted at London, two and a half times as many as at York or Lincoln, and over three times as many as the surviving coins of Winchester (*14.* Petersson 1969, 140–1). During the reign of Edward the Confessor London usually had about twice as many moneyers as Winchester striking any one type (*13.* Dolley 1966, 12–13). If we turn to trade, the picture is not dissimilar. Writing of Norman London Sir Frank Stenton remarked, 'from no other English town have we evidence of so considerable a body of trade at this early date . . . at the beginning of the eleventh century or earlier London was being visited by merchants from just the same countries which are represented there under Henry I' (*5.* Stenton 1960, 199). From Rouen, Flanders, Ponthieu, Normandy, France, from the Empire, from Denmark, trade was already flowing into London, activity which must have required growing wharfage and warehousing along the waterfront (*2.* Page 1923, 137–8). The burgeoning of this commerce should probably be placed in the century of peace between 895 and 982, but the investigation of the archaeological evidence of the riverside deposits between Upper and Lower Thames Street and the present foreshore is essential if this development is to be followed on the basis of evidence rather than speculation. No less than for the Roman period, the waterfront presents a

major challenge for Anglo-Saxon archaeology (**2, 15, 16, 18, 20, 38, 42, 43, 45, 46, 67, 69, 70, 96**).

Anglo-Saxon London: summary
4.47   No excuse is offered for the lengthy attention given here to Anglo-Saxon London. This period is undoubtedly the least known and least understood of London's past, and the archaeological contribution has so far scarcely been brought to bear on its problems. The opportunities are nevertheless considerable, but they will not long remain. It is obvious first that a thorough knowledge of Roman London is essential to any understanding of the physical form and topographical development of the Anglo-Saxon city. Of the areas which require extensive and immediate attention the waterfront must come first. Here alone the archaeological deposits still survive to a reasonable extent, and here should be found evidence for the commercial development of London from the fifth to the eleventh centuries. Of the problems demanding urgent consideration, the area of occupation at various periods, both within and without the walls is particularly pressing. Here it is vital that arrangements should be made for the observation of every disturbance of the ground, and for the recording of structures and the collection of finds. Every opportunity should be taken to observe and investigate the defences, especially the ditch system and the intra-mural street. Investigation of the exceedingly complex problems of the development of London's street pattern should have a high priority. As Jeremy Haslam has recently shown, and as Tom Hassall has demonstrated at Oxford, evidence for early streets can still survive even where a street has been in use until the present and has been heavily disturbed by the insertion of sewers and other services (*10c.* Haslam 1972; *14.* Hassall 1971, 8–9, figs.5 and 6, pl. IIIB). Closely allied is the question of the development of the street markets of Westcheap and Eastcheap, and the relationship of these and other streets to the survival of elements of the Roman street pattern. For all these and many other problems the history of the London churches is of especial interest. While the early history and structural development of an individual church may have a value all of its own, the archaeology of the church in its parish, as an element in the urban scene, and of the churches of the city as a whole, as elements in the growth of the entire community, have a contribution to make to the history and archaeology of London that is of very great potential interest. Unless all these problems receive in the next ten years a degree of attention going far beyond anything that has so far been achieved or even imagined, the history of Anglo-Saxon London,

> *Vrbs est ampla nimis, peruersis plena colonis,*
> *Et regni reliquis dicior est opibus,*

'a great city, overflowing with froward inhabitants, and richer in treasure than the rest of the kingdom', as it was described by Guy of Amiens in 1067, will never be more than a faded vision.*

The archaeology of medieval London

4.48   The problems facing the archaeology of London during the five centuries following the Norman conquest might seem at first sight to be of a quite different order from those of earlier periods (*Map 4*). The sources for the history of the city during these centuries are incomparably richer than those for the Anglo-Saxon period, and they become ever more detailed as the centuries pass. The documentary evidence alone is so extensive that its study for the topographical development of the city has scarcely yet been undertaken on a systematic basis, while there survive from this period major structural monuments which can still be studied at first hand, or at least in a wealth of pictorial records of varying degrees of completeness and accuracy, dating from the sixteenth century onwards. The period is nevertheless a long one, and the sources available for the later eleventh, twelfth or even thirteenth centuries cannot compare with the mass of information accessible for the later medieval period. Even when the existence of a building, its site and outline history are known, its exact position, layout, character and structural development may only be ascertainable by archaeological and architectural-historical investigation in combination with renewed and revised documentary analysis. Most, perhaps all, of the city's medieval churches fall into this category, and notable examples of the success of this approach are to be seen in Professor Grimes's work at St Bride's or at the Charterhouse (*11.* Grimes 1968, 182–97; *5.* Knowles and Grimes, 1954), or in Brian Davison's elucidation of the early development of the Tower (*5.* Hurst 1964, 255, fig.83). More generally, the fact of the occupation of an area, such as a monastic precinct, street frontage, or even a whole quarter like the riverfront, may be known, but nothing at all may be understood in detail, or even in broad outline of the character and sequence of its occupation. The clearest example in this case is the waterfront, where the growth riverwards of the many lanes running south from Upper and Middle Thames Street, and the nature and sequence of the commercial properties flanking them, is entirely unstudied.

4.49   These problems are to some extent specific and could (excluding the waterfront) be regarded as detail subordinate to the overall pattern of the city's growth and changing character. It is something of a surprise to realize that even these broader issues cannot adequately be discussed without archaeologi

cal evidence used in combination with documentary evidence in a mutually beneficial relationship. Archaeology, as will be seen, is as basic to an understanding of these broader issues in the full medieval period, as it must inevitably be (for lack of other evidence) in the pre-conquest period. The extent of the built-up area within the walls, and the growth of the suburbs, cannot be established without archaeological evidence before the fourteenth or perhaps later thirteenth century (*fig.9.5, 9.6*). Alterations to the street plan, whether by the laying out of new streets or the closing of older ones, can normally only be dated by archaeological evidence, perhaps in combination with street-name studies. The evolution of the defences, involving the addition of bastions, alterations to the gates, reformation of the ditches, and even the extension of the walled area at Blackfriars (*11.* Grimes 1968, 52–6), can only be followed, where the evidence survives at all, by archaeology used whenever possible in combination with documentary sources. And the latter may themselves be made to yield fresh and unsuspected information in the light of this new approach. The relationship of religious precincts to the pre-existing properties out of which they were formed, and the nature of this earlier occupation can also only be studied by a similar combined approach (*Map 4*).

4.50   The contribution of archaeology to the study of medieval London is thus potentially of far greater importance than merely as the provider of background information about the material culture and daily life of the city's inhabitants. It is unfortunate that the massive destruction of the medieval levels which has already taken place should have led to the dominance of the well and the cesspit in London's medieval archaeology. The contents of such features, rich in remarkable artefacts as they often are in London, has perhaps given rise to the impression that the medieval archaeology of the City rarely surpasses the merely interesting to come to grips with the wider and more important aspects of urban history. Professor Grimes has shown, however, how much can be achieved when the right questions are asked and the hypotheses put to the test (*11.* Grimes 1968, 64–91, 131–217). The destruction of the medieval levels by medieval and post-medieval constructions has, however, seriously limited the potential of medieval archaeology, if it has not in many places already eliminated it entirely. It is scarcely to be imagined that any extensive study of medieval house types is now possible in the City, although fragments, more or less meaningful, may be recovered from time to time. Only in the riverfront areas, where very deep medieval deposits still survive (*fig.5*) will the investigation of medieval houses, and these perhaps of a special type conditioned by their site and use, still be possible. As many excavations have now shown, the examination

*5. Morton and Muntz 1972, 40–1, lines 637–8.

of church sites, whose importance has been stressed throughout this survey, is likely to be more fruitful despite massive post-medieval disturbance by burials. A reasonable appreciation of the origins and structural development of London's churches does in fact appear to be an attainable objective, towards which good progress has already been made.

4.51   The importance of London's waterfront has been urged so often here that it may not seem necessary to stress yet again that the depth and water-logged nature of the deposits still surviving will have a major contribution to make to a knowledge of London's trade connexions at home and abroad, her manufactures, and the details of her daily life in the medieval period, as in earlier periods. The success that has already attended Peter Marsden's work on the remains of early ships near the foreshore suggests that contributions to nautical archaeology would not be the least valuable result of greatly intensified and properly conducted excavations in this area (*3*. Marsden 1967*b*; *11*. Marsden 1971). Medieval ships and ships' tackle clearly await discovery in the water-logged deposits along the river. Indeed the neglect of the archaeology of London's waterfront is difficult to comprehend since the potential of such excavations has for many years been well known in this country as a result of the work in a closely comparable situation on the medieval *Bryggen* at Bergen (*14*. Herteig 1959, 1969).

4.52   It is clear that intensive investigation into the archaeology of medieval London needs to be planned and conducted within a framework of renewed and extensive research on the documentary sources for the topography of the medieval city. The concentration of medieval historians has so far been on the institutions and government of the city, on the ruling and merchant classes, and on economic history (e.g. *5*. Thrupp 1962; *5*. Williams 1963). This is natural and essential. By contrast, topographical studies have perhaps tended to be antiquarian rather than academic, concerned with individual entities rather than overall patterns and quantitative approaches. The physical reality of the medieval city as an urban phenomenon has not yet been grasped, although this is possibly the result of the almost overwhelming mass of information available concerning the properties of the medieval city, than because the need has not been realized. The topography of medieval London needs never-

theless to be studied on the lines pioneered by H. E. Salter at Oxford, and now being carried forward much more intensively by D. J. Keene for the entire area of medieval Winchester (*14*. Keene 1972). A notable pioneering effort by Miss M. B. Honeybourne presents, in her words 'A sketch map of London under Richard II' (*8*. Honeybourne 1960, 1965), but the full potential of this approach can only be reached by tracing the history of each property throughout its recorded history, and by the preparation of a sequence of property maps, which can in turn form the basis for an appreciation of the changing social and economic geography of the medieval city. This is an immense task, but its value will be widely recognized, and would not be least in the insights it could provide for the planning and interpretation of archaeological work in the medieval city. Indeed a thorough documentary study of individual sites will be vital for properly conducted archaeological investigation, and for this reason alone a historian will be an essential member of any future City of London Archaeological Unit (*7. 11*). But such a full-scale topographical investigation as that outlined here has a value entirely of its own, which quite transcends the purely 'service' element, however essential, in a properly composed archaeological team.

4.53   The priorities in the archaeological investigation of medieval London appear to be closely similar to those for the earlier periods (*4.19, 47*). The growth in the extent of the occupied area requires the constant observation of all disturbances of the ground, the recording of information and the collection of datable finds. The techniques which have been used to establish by distribution maps the extent of the early Roman nucleus (*4.10*) could as well be applied to study of the growth of the medieval suburbs, or of the increase in the occupied area within the walls (*fig.9.5, 9.6*). Streets need to be observed in section and archaeologically investigated wherever possible. The defences still provide many problems, and no opportunity should be missed to investigate the sites of medieval churches, or the areas adjacent to them. Much has still to be learnt of the great religious precincts (*Map 4*), while as for every other period the potential and requirements of the archaeology of the waterfront present remarkable opportunities as well as the requisite of large-scale excavation, and its associated research and publication.

5 The survival of the evidence for London's past

The depth of archaeological deposits

5.1   To obtain any accurate idea of the extent to which archaeological deposits still survive in the City, and the degree to which they will be affected by any proposed development, it is necessary to know both the depth of the deposits and the depth of existing or proposed underground constructions. The available evidence concerning the depth of archaeological deposits is shown on *Map 6*, summarized in *fig.5*. An indication of the extent to which these deposits have already been destroyed by underground constructions is provided by *Map 5*, summarized in *fig.6*.

5.2   The depth of archaeological deposits varies greatly over the area of the ancient walled city and its immediate surroundings. The land surface was irregular at the commencement of permanent settlement *c.*A.D.43, and the passage of twenty centuries has not succeeded in completely obscuring the original relief. To establish the potential depth of archaeological deposits below today's streets, a contour map of the variations in the original ground surface must be constructed (*3.* Marsden 1972). This shows the two hills on which London stands, Cornhill to the east and Ludgate Hill to the west, each rising to 11 or 12 metres above Ordnance Datum (*Map 6*). The ground falls steeply to the Thames, and into the Walbrook Valley which lies between the two hills, but runs off rather less steeply into the Fleet Valley to the west. In Roman times the relief was even more marked, for the Thames seems to have been 3 or 4 metres lower at average high spring tides than it is today.

5.3   *Map 6* also shows the observed depth or thickness of archaeological deposits at about 160 spots throughout the City. This information has come from archaeological excavations, and from the inspection of building sites, and shows the depth below pavement level (in a few cases, below basement level at that point) of the undisturbed natural sub-soil of London. Put another way, these observations indicate the extent to which, at a series of given points, human activity through 2,000 years has raised the surface of the ground by the repeated deposition of refuse and building materials. These archaeological layers or deposits reach their greatest depth of between 7 and 8 metres near the highest point of Cornhill and in the deepest part of the Walbrook Valley. The depth is between 5 and 6 metres in places on the western hill, and is almost everywhere over 4 metres along the Thames. Only on the slopes down to the Thames and Walbrook, where occupation may have tended to cause less accumulation of soil, and where the archaeological layers may have been subject to natural erosion, or in the peripheral parts of the walled area, are the deposits less deep. These observations are summarized on *fig.5*, which shows areas where the archaeological layers are of roughly equal depth. This figure emphasizes the depth of deposits in the Walbrook Valley and notably along the Thames frontage. While it is obvious that much more information is needed in nearly all areas, especially south and west of St. Paul's and on the south-eastern slopes of Cornhill, the picture already available makes it possible to judge reasonably well the extent to which an existing or proposed underground construction has or will affect the archaeological deposits.

The present extent of survival

5.4   The extent to which the archaeology of the City still survives below ground can only be ascertained through an understanding of the structural requirements of the City's commercial activities. The City plays a unique role as the core area for Britain's financial transactions. Head offices of British firms and branches of international firms have sought locations near to the Bank of England and the commodity markets. It is particularly the banking, insurance and other financial firms that have, for various reasons, concentrated in the City within an area of about 1.5 kilometres to east and west of the Bank of England. The wholesale and commodity markets, shipping, and the printing and publishing industry form with these financial firms the chief occupiers of premises. The pace of redevelopment must continue at a high rate in order to meet the requirements of these firms both for space and for standard of accommodation. It was suggested in

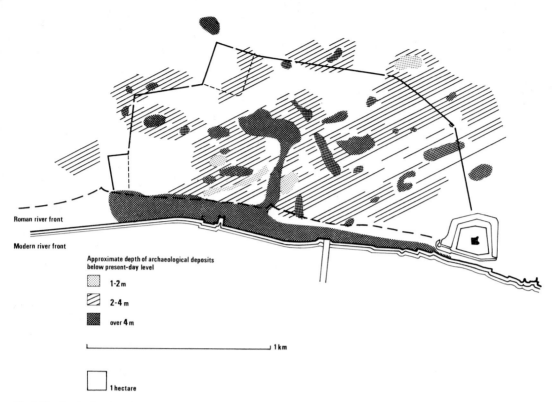

Roman river front

Modern river front

Approximate depth of archaeological deposits below present-day level

1-2 m

2-4 m

over 4 m

1 km

1 hectare

Fig.5 The depth of archaeological deposits in the City : a summary (1 : 20,000). *Compare Map 6*

1947 that about a quarter of all buildings in the City were rebuilt on average in a span of thirty years. By 1905 80% of the buildings that existed in 1855 had been rebuilt, and about 20% of the buildings existing in 1905 had been rebuilt by 1939. Most of the buildings erected between 1901 and 1939 were built on a more substantial scale, using steel frames necessitating greater destruction of the ground. During the war approximately 91 hectares (225 acres) were destroyed and much of this area was of older buildings which were swept by fire. The more substantial modern buildings withstood the bombing more easily. In the immediate post-war years there were six areas of extensive war damage (*fig.1*). Between the major area which extended from the present Barbican area south to the river between Blackfriars and London Bridge, and the areas north from Tower Hill and north of St Helen's Place, there remained an area in which many developments had probably already destroyed the underlying archaeological layers. Following the Town and Country Planning Act 1944, the City was given authority to acquire the extensively war-damaged areas and any adjoining property, and to plan and redevelop these areas as a whole. Thus it was possible to lay out new streets unrestricted by former patterns of land ownership, which could be very complex. The reconstruction of these war-damaged areas has in most cases probably destroyed the archaeological levels, although pockets may survive from place to place, as well as the lower parts of the deeper features, such as pits and wells (*4.50*). Three large precinct developments have taken place over the post-war years

on parts of the damaged areas. The major project was the Barbican, which consists of 15.2 hectares of residential development and a commercial zone of 11.3 hectares. The area to the north of St Paul's has been laid out with office blocks and pedestrian squares, and the Tower of London precinct includes shops, restaurant facilities and car parking accommodation for visiting tourists, as well as office space. In these three areas the Corporation acquired and developed the land, providing for a considerable reduction in commercial floor space and day-time population. Although these new buildings could have a longer life structurally than their predecessors, the pace of functional obsolescence is increasing. It seems unlikely that their life span will in fact greatly exceed that of earlier structures (*cf.5.15* note).

5.5   The only method of quantifying the archaeological implications of the developments outlined in the last paragraph is to find some method of mapping the extent of below-ground structures. It appeared that this could only be achieved through a building by building inquiry, which was obviously not practicable, but early in our work it emerged that Messrs Chas. Goad Ltd had been compiling an analogous survey at regular intervals since the last century, for insurance purposes. The categories used in their surveys do not always lend themselves to an easy definition of the basements concerned, and some basements are omitted, for reasons which are not immediately obvious. The areas outlined (but not shaded or filled in) on *Map 5*

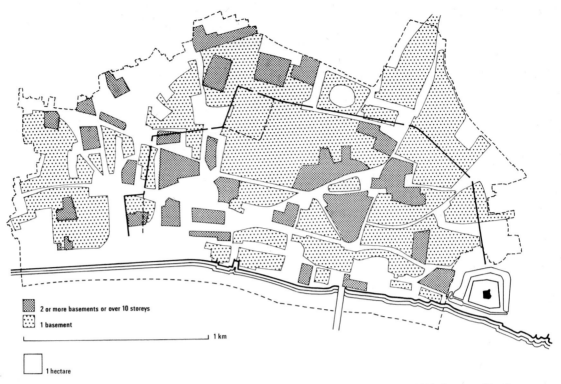

Fig.6 The state of archaeological deposits in the City : a summary of basement depths (1 : 20,000). *Compare Map 5*

show those substantial buildings in the Goad survey which are not specifically listed as having basements, but which are known in many cases to possess them. In spite of its imperfections for the present purpose (for which it was not compiled), this survey provides the only available index of the destruction of London's archaeological deposits by underground structures. We are therefore deeply indebted to Messrs Chas. Goad for permission to base *Map 5* on their latest survey, which covers developments up to

1970, but which has since been discontinued. The course of cut-and-cover underground railways, and major junction and low-level station constructions are also shown on *Map 5*, which is summarized in a simplified form in *fig.6*.

5.6   The land area within the administrative boundaries of the City is approximately 677 acres (274 hectares). The following figures emerge from *Map 5*:

Table I★

Two or more basements	125 acres	⎫
		⎬ Total archaeological destruction
Cut-and-cover railways	42	⎭
One basement	51	⎫
One basement or deep foundations	105	⎬ Partial archaeological destruction
Streets	236	⎭
	559 acres	
Remainder	118	Archaeological state unknown
Total	677 acres (plus 62 acres water)	

These figures relate to the whole area of the modern administrative City and County, and not to the walled area alone, but archaeological deposits are likely to be encountered anywhere within these boundaries, and being shallower in the peripheral areas, will have been more seriously disturbed by shallower developments. Furthermore, since the Goad survey is known to be neither quite complete

nor revised beyond 1970, it is clear that in this respect also the situation is under- rather than over-estimated. Nearly 170 acres (69 hectares), or 25% of the City of London appears from these figures to

★The figures in the tables are given in imperial acres as in the sources from which they were derived. Where they are repeated in the body of the text, their metric equivalents are also quoted.

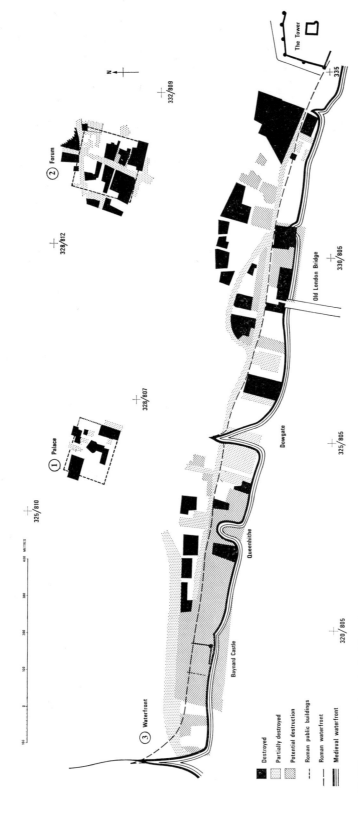

Fig. 7 The state of archaeological deposits in the City: sample areas (1 : 10,000). 1, the so-called Roman governor's palace in the area of Bush Lane and Cannon Street Station ; 2, the Roman forum and basilica in the area of Gracechurch Street ; 3, the waterfront from the Fleet to the Tower

have been archaeologically destroyed by 1970, and a further 392 acres (159 hectares), 58% to have been at least partially damaged, usually with extensive or total loss of the medieval, and sometimes even the late Roman layers.

5.7   If the incidence of the deeper basements is considered, it will be seen that it conforms quite closely to the core of the financial district discussed in 5.4 to the east and west of the Bank of England. The double basements – they are frequently much deeper – covering the greater part of Cornhill must mean that most of the archaeology of the nucleus of early Roman London has already been destroyed. The St Paul's area has been almost as severely affected. Except in the Barbican area, most of the deeper basements are within the walled area, and even if the greater depth of archaeological deposits on Cornhill and Ludgate Hill are taken into account, by reading *Map 6* over *Map 5*, it will still be seen that the double basements can normally be regarded as having totally destroyed the archaeological deposits in their area.

5.8   Examples of survival and destruction are given in *fig. 7*. In the case of the two principal known public buildings of Roman London, the 'governor's palace' (*fig.7.1*), and the forum-basilica complex (*fig.7.2*), total destruction can be seen to account for about half the area of each, with partial destruction accounting for at least another quarter of the forum. The incidence of known future disturbance of both these sites is at present relatively slight, but takes on much greater importance in view of the destruction they have already undergone.

5.9   A striking contrast is provided by the *present* condition of the water front (*fig.7.3*). This is the one area of deep archaeological deposits not so far affected by correspondingly deep modern constructions. This is the exact opposite of the situation on Cornhill and Ludgate Hill, and would seem only to be matched by parts of the Walbrook valley (cf. *figs.5* and *6*). The waterfront is 1,900 m. in length from the Fleet to the Tower. Of this length at the middle of 1972 only some 300 m., 16% had so far been affected by double basements (and hence archaeologically destroyed), while only a further 140 m., 7·8% had been partly damaged. Work now begun at the western end of the area at Baynard Castle, or scheduled to begin in the immediate future elsewhere along the river, will affect a further 750 m., 39% of the waterfront, and will in most cases totally remove or very seriously disturb archaeological deposits which are at present essentially intact. This threat in one of the very few, if not the only, reasonably well preserved areas of archaeological deposits in the City of London would be

serious, even if the area were not of quite exceptional importance for the history of the City (*4.14, 17, 38, 46, 51*).

5.10   As with the waterfront, it is only when the existing position is seen in the light of proposed developments that any picture of the total situation emerges. From the figures given in Table I (*5.6*), it appears that there are 118 acres (48 hectares) in the City whose archaeological 'status' is unknown. This is 17% of the total land area. It must not be assumed that it is all archaeologically intact. It includes 22 acres (9 hectares) of open spaces (Table V, *5.14*), to which must be added the sites of the city churches themselves, whether in use or ruined (*Map 7*). It must also include some vacant space (with no basements, or filled-in basements), and will, finally, comprise a few areas still archaeologically intact. *Map 5* suggests that these lie in the peripheral areas, either along the waterfront, or outside the city wall.

The future extent of destruction

5.11   Since the last war the Government has introduced legislation to control industrial and office developments in an attempt to decentralize activities from congested central areas and to spread employment opportunities to less prosperous regions. The Control of Office and Industrial Development Act 1965 has been of most significance to developers in the City, where the floor space taken by offices in place of industry or commerce has been increasing since the war. Although the Corporation has attempted to plan for some return of the residential population, this has only been possible in high cost schemes. Areas of commercial use have suffered both from the disadvantages of congestion and from the movement downstream of London's port activities. Dockland areas beyond the City's boundaries are at present facing the problems of redevelopment, for example Hay's Wharf and the 5,000 acres (2,000 odd hectares) studied to the east of the Tower, and it may be questioned what effects plans in these areas will have on the City of London. Within the City much of the riverside area is being developed or faces development in the future, while other commercial areas are under pressure. For example, the PLA warehouses north of Houndsditch have already had an office redevelopment scheme mooted now that the warehouses are no longer required.

5.12   The operation of the Government's ODP (Office Development Permit) policy probably succeeds in restricting developments to those by firms which have strong reasons for seeking a central site, but there is controversy as to whether the policy is too restrictive and keeps away firms which could be economically justified in a central location. Refusals of ODPs generally total about one-third to one-quarter the approvals, although some schemes may be modified and resubmitted successfully after a first refusal (Table II). Once the developer has an ODP it would appear that the refusal rate from the Corporation is fairly low (Table III: no breakdown according to use is given in this table), and that there is a predominance of office uses receiving planning permission for new development or change of use (Table IV).

Table II
Applications for ODPs in the City, 1965–70

	Permits	Refusals
1965 (Aug.–Dec.)	8	13
1966	9	4
1967	12	6
1968	28	6
1969	49	17
1970	80	18

Source: Ministry of Housing and Local Government, from 9. Dunning and Morgan 1971

Table III
Planning applications for the City of London, 1966–70

	Permits	Refusals
1966	341	12
1967	271	9
1968	317	6
1969	305	7
1970	255	12

N.B. This table includes all planning applications received, including those for extensions and limited period permissions.
Source: 9. GLC 1966–70 (5(1970))

5.13 At the present time office rents have risen to a general level of £10 per sq. ft. It has been suggested that in the future many firms are likely to consider a move to a decentralized location or to the fringes of the City, if this is not too detrimental to their operation, rather than pay a higher rent. There is evidence that a prestige address is of declining importance, and a location within a mile or two of the centre may possibly be more attractive if the rent is lower. Within the next five years one may predict that the fringe areas, for example around Liverpool Street Station and Aldgate, will attract developers, although it is uncertain what relative rent level will be prevalent. However, there will continue to be a demand for the really central sites from those firms which require proximity to the financial and commodity markets, and which depend on what has been termed 'knowledge in a hurry'. Both the central sites and peripheral offices are likely to require redevelopment of existing premises when these become inadequate for their requirements. The age of buildings becomes relevant in this context and may serve as an indicator of areas where redevelopment is likely, although not yet officially mooted (*Map 7*), especially when considered in the light of the general trends governing renewal of the building stock of the City (*5.4*). Nevertheless, in central prestige sites the pressure to provide modern air-conditioned, open-plan offices may act just as powerfully on buildings of the earlier twentieth century, as on nineteenth-century buildings in more peripheral areas. Age of buildings may not therefore be a reliable indicator of all areas of future redevelopment.

5.14 Since the war and up to September 1972 about 196 acres (79 hectares) have had redevelopments completed. This figure includes the Barbican site, which is still under construction. At Sepember 1972 a further 15–16 acres (6 hectares) were under construction, and a total of 212 acres (86 hectares) has thus been affected by redevelopment during the period. When compared with an acreage of 441 (178 hectares) within street blocks, it is apparent that the possibilities for archaeology are rapidly diminishing.

Table IV
Planning permissions granted

	1965	1966	1967	1968	1969	1970	1971
Commerce	8	9	11	7	7	4	1
Industry	1	6	1	6	6	2	0
Offices	29	36	30	41	69	60	81
Total*	52	82	64	62	96	80	101

*N.B. totals include other uses, and there may also be double counting of sites which include, e.g., both industry and offices
Figures cover new development, change of use, and outline permissions only
Source: GLC Decisions Analysis

Areas where development is
likely in the next 5 years

Areas to be developed
in the near future

1 km

1 hectare

Fig.8 The future of archaeological deposits in the City : a summary of impending development (1 :20,000)

Table V
Site acreage of different uses, 1966

Offices	211
Vacant	90
Water	62
Commerce	36
Open areas	22
Public Buildings	20
Shops	18
Industry	14
Transport, utilities	10
Residential	8
Health	8
Education	4
Sub-total	503
Streets	236
Total acreage City★	739

★Including 62 acres water
Source: 9. GLC 1972

Much of the remaining acreage has already been entirely or partially destroyed by the large office blocks, some incorporating two or three basements, that are found in the central banking district. In 1966 there were 36 acres (15 hectares) of commercial uses and 14 acres (6 hectares) of industry, compared with 211 acres (85 hectares) of office use (Table V). Of the 90 acres (36 hectares) of vacant land, 53 acres (21 hectares) were construction sites and only 3 acres (1.2 hectares) derelict. The acreage unaccounted for in these figures (236 acres, 95.5 hectares) is made up of roads, of which there are 33 miles (53 kilometres) in the City.

5.15   *Map 8*, summarized in *fig.8*, shows that there are considerable areas of the City for which there are permissions outstanding or where there is evidence of the possibility of redevelopment in the short term (see Appendix I, schedule, for full details). In general, the permissions that are granted in the central heart of the City (about 750 metres to either side of the Bank and between Cannon Street and London Wall) are put into effect very soon after they are made. The peripheral schemes, where the economic pressures are less, may remain outstanding for a number of years. Over this time alternative proposals may be put forward. The areas shown in black as areas of probable future development are in many cases areas outstanding from the proposals made in the LCC Development Plan of 1962. Such areas are generally mixed areas of

33

obsolescent buildings.* The Ludgate Circus area has been awaiting development since the war, but uncertainties of road proposals and the future of the railway viaduct have held up development. For the areas south-west of St Paul's various different schemes have been prepared. At the present time this area is within one of the GLC Development Plan action areas. There are three such areas within the City for which the Corporation is responsible for preparing reports and making any necessary suggestions for development. The Barbican Action Area is the smallest of these and involves modernization to provide for pedestrian and vehicular circulation. The Monument, and the St Paul's South-West Action Areas are both varied in composition. The latter is of particular importance because of its proximity to St Paul's and its position north of the North Bank redevelopment area. Many of the buildings are obsolescent and part of the area, not having been touched since the war, still lies in ruins. However, within the Action Area there are ten listed buildings and a Conservation Area.

---

*Also included on *Map 8* and in the Schedule in Appendix I are some sites where permission has been refused. In such cases it will probably be only a matter of time before the development does go through in a modified form. The age of buildings gives some guide to the areas which will need redevelopment on ground of age and obsolescence (*Map 7*). In some cases these buildings may be protected if they are substantial landmarks or if they are of enough architectural value to make internal alterations a viable proposition. It must also be noted that modern buildings are not necessarily secure from the developer. New Fresh Wharf, built in the early 1950s, is to be redeveloped in the Billingsgate Market scheme: Appendix I, no.69.

Billingsgate also has problems of obsolescence and traffic congestion.

5.16   The designation of Conservation Areas under the Civic Amenities Act 1967 does not necessarily protect these areas from redevelopment (*Map 8*). The Act places on the Local Planning Authority the task of designating such areas of special architectural or historic interest, and of protecting or improving these areas if they so wish. Developments should enhance the area and action may be taken to improve groups of buildings. These measures should deter any radical redevelopments, and all applications must be published in the local press as well as on or near the land to which they relate. Thus the public has the opportunity to make representations. In deciding on the application the Local Planning Authority, or the Minister, must pay special attention to the character and appearance of the area. The recent proposals by a property company to redevelop the Victorian parts of Wardrobe Place in the St Andrew's Hill Conservation Area is one instance where controversy has arisen over the merits of a new building which might enhance the appearance but might alter the character of the area. In the Bow Lane Area there are three schemes, one of which is already under way. Such schemes may not destroy the area architecturally. Along Bow Lane Nos.49–51 have been rebuilt, but retain the intimate scale of the narrow Lane. However, archaeological layers were probably destroyed in the process. The listing of buildings is a more positive restraint on development. To demolish such a building it is necessary for the developer to apply for a listed

Table VI
Listed Building Consents

A. To alter or extend	Applications	Permissions	Refusals
1968	16	★	★
1969	5	5	—
1970	2	2	—
1971	17	16	1
B. To demolish			
1968	4	★	★
1969	2	—	—
1970	7	5	1
1971	6	1	5

★No figure given.
N.B. Where the permissions and refusals do not add up to the total applications, cases may have been held over for ministerial decision
Source: City of London Department of Architecture and Planning

building consent and if this is granted time must be given for a record of the building to be made in drawings and photographs. The City has lost a relatively large number of listed buildings in the past, but it seems possible that the situation is changing. After public inquiries the Minister has refused permission in the case of the Old Shades Wine House, the façade and main building of the National Provincial Bank, and the George & Vulture (Table VI). Under the Town and Country Planning (Amendment) Act 1972 the local planning authority has powers to direct that the demolition of certain non-listed buildings in a Conservation Area should be subject to control. This offers some protection to buildings which are of value to the character or appearance of an area without having the individual significance to merit listing.

5.17 The emphasis of development in the City of London is moving away from the central areas, where so much has been done since the war, to the more peripheral areas to the west and north-east, and to the entire length of the waterfront (*fig. 8*). The schedule in Appendix I shows that 131 sites are currently under consideration or outstanding from earlier years. In eighty-eight cases action is expected in the near future. In the remaining forty-three cases it seems likely that development will take place within the next five years. In the twenty-seven years between 1945 and 1972, 212 acres (86 hectares) were developed out of an acreage within the street blocks of 441 (178 hectares: *5.14*). With ODPs now increasing rapidly each year (Table II), and the granting of planning permissions showing a steady rise (Table IV), it seems obvious that the remaining built-up areas will be redeveloped considerably faster than in the last twenty-five years. Some of the individual developments are on a very large scale. There remain 229 acres (93 hectares), of the 441 acres within the street blocks, not developed since the Second World War. The actual area still available for redevelopment, without beginning again on sites aready once rebuilt since the war, must however be much smaller. For the 229 acres include all the public buildings and church sites as well as most of the public open spaces, a total of about 42 acres (17 hectares: Table V). There cannot therefore be more than about 190 acres (77 hectares) to be redeveloped. At today's tempo this process will not take more than twenty years, and more probably fifteen years or even less. When this process is complete very little of London's archaeology will be left, except in some of the 22 acres (9 hectares) of open space, below the churches, and in a few other pockets. It will not be enough to make any kind of historical sense.

6 The present position: an assessment

The major problems

6.1   There are two main sets of problems confronting London's archaeology. The one, academic, setting out the main areas of uncertainty both chronological and topographical will be dealt with in this chapter. The other, administrative, covering problems of organization and finance, will be discussed in *Chapter 7*.

6.2   The site of the City has now been permanently occupied for something over nineteen hundred years (*4.1*). There is no period before the thirteenth century for which we possess a tolerable understanding of the city's evolution and character, and even during the later middle ages there are many matters awaiting further investigation by documentary and archaeological research (*4.48–53*). Only perhaps with the sixteenth century, and the coming of the first maps and views, do we reach a period where our knowledge of the physical character of the city rests on a reasonably secure foundation. In the first thirteen centuries of London's existence, during a long sequence of periods whose most constant feature is our inadequate comprehension of their real nature, certain epochs stand out as areas of almost total ignorance. As a result of the uneven emphasis of archaeological research (*fig.4*), the period from the fifth to the eleventh centuries must be regarded as the least known in the whole of London's past (*4.20–47*). The origins of the city are almost equally obscure, the darkness relieved only by our ability to see London in the wider context of the birth of Roman Britain (*4.10, 11*). A comparable background for the study of Anglo-Saxon London is only now emerging, and a first attempt has been made in these pages to see what this implies for the development of the city itself (*4.23*). Selection may be invidious where so little is known of any of these earlier periods, but the problem of the Anglo-Saxon city seems nevertheless to merit especial consideration, *primus inter pares*.

6.3   The particular problems facing the archaeology of the main periods of London's past have been discussed and summarized above (*4.19, 47* and *53*). From this discussion certain aspects have emerged

that are common to more than one, or to all periods. The expansion and contraction of the occupied area within the walls, and the origins and growth of the extra-mural suburbs, form perhaps the single most important question affecting all periods: the size of the city. Within this larger framework, the initiation and subsequent development of commercial activity on the Thames waterfront provides an issue of crucial importance to any understanding of the economic life of the city at its successive periods (*4.14, 17, 29, 38, 46* and *51*). Of the separate components of the City's pattern, the bridge, the defences, the streets and the churches are likely to offer information regarding the development of the city going far beyond the importance of an individual site. Investigation of the Cripplegate fort and of the city wall of the early third century A.D. provide almost the only examples of a planned programme of excavation in London's archaeology, but the earlier stages of the Roman defences are unknown (*4.13*), and much still remains to be learnt of the Anglo-Saxon and medieval walls and gates. By contrast, study of the street-pattern has barely started. Yet it is in the origin, use, decay or survival of the Roman streets, and in the emergence of new lines and patterns at various dates during the Anglo-Saxon and medieval periods that some of the most important information will be found regarding the overall development of the city in successive periods (*4.13, 36, 41–3* and *47*). Study of the cemeteries of the Roman city, and of the origins of intra- and extra-mural churches in the Anglo-Saxon and later periods should also supply fresh information of great importance for the evolution of the city as a whole (*4.15, 18, 29, 37, 44, 45* and *48*). Such a concentration as thus seems necessary to establish the broad outlines of London's topographical evolution will also bear on the problem of the continuity of occupation in the post-Roman period, or, more precisely on the nature of this occupation, for the fact of continuous occupation of some kind seems no longer in doubt historically (*4.17, 18* and *24–28*).

6.4   This survey has been mainly concerned with the history and archaeology of London up to the end of the middle ages. It must not be thought that London's archaeology ends with the dawning of the early modern period. The excavations in recent years at Fulham, and on the South Bank in Lambeth and Southwark have shown, if any proof were needed, that such a view would be a travesty of reality. But the post-medieval archaeology of the City presents very great problems. It has undoubtedly been even more seriously damaged than that of any other period, and is likely in most cases to appear only in the fillings of pits and wells. No period can be adequately studied on such evidence alone, and in a period where the evidence of archaeology and of written sources must be carefully composed and counterpointed, it cannot be claimed that the post-medieval archaeology of the City itself can ever have a large role to play. It is essential, however, on all sites excavated, that the early modern occupation of the site should be carefully studied from documentary sources before excavation begins, so that the chance survival of post-medieval deposits can be fully exploited against a background knowledge of the kind of use to which the site has been put in recent centuries. If the information to emerge, except in technological fields such as potting, glass making, or metal working, is likely to appear secondary in importance to the written sources, it is nevertheless probably of a quite different character and otherwise unobtainable. It should not be ignored.

6.5 This survey has also been restricted to the administrative area of the City and County of the City of London (*Map 1*, etc.). This means that the survey has been essentially, as was intended, a survey of the ancient walled city and its immediate environs. The important settlement of Southwark has not been included, except in a few entries in the bibliography (*Appendix III, 2, 10e* and *11*), and for completeness in *fig.9*, where some suggestions have been made concerning the Anglo-Saxon burh, based on the relief of the ground and on possible early street-lines and other topographical features. Nor has Westminster been included, or development along Fleet Street and the Strand in the middle ages. The City cannot, however, be studied in isolation from its surroundings, a point which Ralph Merrifield has made abundantly clear in his account of the setting of Roman London (*3.* Merrifield 1969, 28–67, 133–46), and which has also emerged at various stages in this survey (e.g., *4.25–7*). Likewise there can be no reason for developing the archaeology of the City at the expense of the less immediately striking but historically equally essential investigation of the archaeology of the surrounding Greater London area. Whether or not the archaeology of the City and of Greater London is to be administered as a single unit (*7.14*), both areas must receive adequate attention. Many phases of the city's evolution cannot be understood without a knowledge of the situation in the city's hinterland. It is

equally obvious that the hinterland cannot be studied without a knowledge of the city.

6.6 There can be no doubt that growth in understanding of the City's past has been seriously hindered by the failure to publish in detail the results of previous work. All credit must be given to Guildhall Museum and its staff, especially Peter Marsden, for the brief reports that appeared regularly from 1960 to 1970 in the *Transactions of the London and Middlesex Archaeological Society*, and to Professor Grimes for the account of his work in *The Excavation of Roman and Mediaeval London* published in 1968. We have, however, very few proper reports, complete with plans, sections, and a detailed presentation of the finds. Not only does this mean that much basic material is unavailable, it also means that much of it has never been worked over for publication and its implications made apparent even to the excavators or observers themselves. The absence of this material has also inhibited the formulation and discussion of new hypotheses, as well as restricting the impact of London's own contribution on the archaeology of the country as a whole. This situation is not unique to London. The conduct of major excavations, without parallel consideration of the need for money and manpower to prepare the results for publication, was a deplorable feature of British archaeology in the fifties and sixties (*3.10*). In the case of London, the situation has become a major academic problem, and hence its consideration here as well as in *Chapter 7 (7.4f)*. An appreciation of all the information already available from archaeological work in London is essential for the planning of future research within (or indeed without) the rescue programme. Any new organization dealing with the archaeology of the City must therefore make provision not only for the full and rapid publication of its own results, but also for the analysis and publication of all previous unpublished material, particularly the long and important series of observations carried out by Guildhall Museum since 1949 or even 1939 (*3.5, 15*). In the meantime, a map and gazetteer of the archaeology of Anglo-Saxon and medieval London, on the lines of Ralph Merrifield's, *The Roman City of London*, published in 1965, would serve to stimulate fresh research and interest in the manner of its admirable predecessor.

Can the problems still be solved?

6.7 If we return now to the major archaeological problems outlined from the chronological and topographical standpoints in paragraphs *6.2* and *6.3*, we must ask whether these problems can in fact still be resolved, given the great destruction of the evidence which has already taken place, and if so, how this may be achieved and within what kind of time-scale the solutions must be found. This last point will be discussed in a separate section (*6.14–18*).

6.8   Taking the chronological approach first (*cf.* *6.2*), it must certainly seem that the uppermost, and therefore the later, archaeological levels will have suffered most severely from the construction of even comparatively shallow foundations for more recent buildings. That these levels are in fact the medieval levels implies that the process whereby the level of a plot built up period by period in the course of use and reconstruction ceased at some point in time, and was replaced by a more sophisticated approach in which site levels were maintained from period to period, in conformity with surrounding streets and buildings, or were even reduced by the construction of cellars as an increasingly standard procedure. The date of this change in London has not been discussed, but should be broadly ascribed to the seventeenth century, perhaps essentially to the period of reconstruction following the Great Fire. Such a situation would account both for the lack of built-up deposits of the early modern period, as well as for the extensive destruction of the medieval levels, unprotected as they are by a covering of later layers. The medieval deposits have in fact suffered very severely in all ordinary areas of occupation, probably to the extent that there can be little hope of useful results in, for example, the study of medieval house types by excavation. This situation does not always extend to individual masonry buildings such as churches, or religious houses, but it must be expected that in general the medieval deposits of London's past are more severely damaged than those of any other period.

6.9   It is often said that late Roman and Anglo-Saxon layers have suffered very serious destruction from pit digging in the middle ages. The effect of this is particularly serious on Roman buildings, which would not normally on a Roman site be heavily disturbed by Roman pits, but which in a medieval town are frequently eroded to a surprising extent by medieval pits and wells. This impact is even more serious in excavations of limited extent, while its effect can perhaps be minimized in larger excavations where the destruction wrought by later disturbances will not loom so large in the total picture. Being the most deeply buried deposits in the City, the Roman levels are the most protected and will tend to survive relatively more intact than those of later periods. Even under deep basements, the earliest Roman layers and the deeper Roman (and indeed later) pits may still survive intact. This is a possibility that can rarely be ignored, except where existing basements are known to penetrate far below the level of the natural subsoil.

6.10   There can be no doubt that Anglo-Saxon deposits are the most elusive in London's past. For this there are several reasons: their destruction by later medieval activity, their restriction in the earlier Saxon period to a part only of the walled area, their relatively slight nature, and the comparative lack of attention that has been accorded to them. One explanation, that they do not and never did exist on any scale is unacceptable, as the tenor of the historical evidence makes clear (*4.23, 28, 35* and *45*). The real reason for the difficulty in identifying them probably rests in the fact that for this period more than for any other the layers derive from occupation of timber buildings with simple earth floors only rarely improved by the laying of chalk or clay surfaces. The growth of archaeological deposits derives more than anything else from the importation of building materials and the redistribution of soil from the excavation of pits and foundations. If for any reason these activities are restricted, or the pits regularly back-filled, the growth of deposits is hindered. Excavation of Anglo-Saxon town sites elsewhere in the country, for example at Southampton (Hamwih) or Winchester, has shown that several centuries of occupation of this kind may produce less than 50 cm of deposit, and this frequently an undifferentiated dark soil in which individual features can be traced, if at all, only with difficulty. Only after these levels have been removed is it possible to trace the features of this period cut into the underlying levels. Such a deposit, itself cut and partly destroyed by later pits, would be difficult to identify and its underlying features virtually impossible to interpret in the excavations of limited area which have so far been all that has usually been possible in London. It is the nature of the Anglo-Saxon deposits that has probably rendered their discovery so difficult in these already difficult conditions.

6.11   If we pass now to consider the major problem's of London's archaeology from a topographical view-point it can immediately be seen that about one-quarter of the City's surface has been so extensively destroyed by the construction of deep basements that very little archeological evidence can survive intact in these areas (*5.6, Table I*). The situation is especially serious on Cornhill, where the greater part of the hill-top on which London began has now been removed by very deep basements (*5.7, Map 5*). Here, where the archaeological deposits are at their deepest, something should however survive on those sites where the basements are of only one level. But a comparison of *Maps 5* and *7* or *8* will show the extent to which proposed development in this area will fill in the relatively less damaged areas between the existing deep basements. In this critical area, where there have so far been few excavations (*4.8*), the opportunities are becoming fewer every year. They will vanish within the foreseeable future.

6.12   Particular examples of destruction and survival have been given in *fig.7* (cf. *5.8*) and other cases can be established by comparing the maps of basement depth and proposed development (*Maps 5* and *8*) with those of the various historical periods (*Maps 2–4*). Comparison with *Map 6*, showing the depth of archeological deposits, will reveal other factors. In some areas, such as the Cripplegate Fort, the deposits are relatively shallow and destruction by existing buildings correspondingly greater. In other areas, such as parts of the Walbrook valley or the Thames waterfront, the deposits are at their deepest (*fig.5*), and existing structures appear to have caused relatively less disturbance. It is clear from these maps that archaeological sites do still survive scattered all over the city, even if subject to the general points made in *6.8–10*. Many archeological problems can still therefore be approached, even if the answers from these sites may often be incomplete. Unfortunately for archaeology, the maps show a high degree of correlation between such sites and the location of developments proposed for the next five years.

6.13   Although the archaeological evidence has been extensively damaged, and the surviving areas appear to be threatened with a similar fate in the near future, the discussion shows that much can still be done to examine the major problems summarized in *6.2* and *6.3*, and set out in greater detail in *Chapter 4*. Whatever administrative arrangements may prove suitable (*7.5–15*), the following operations will be required:

(*a*) The complete excavation of a few selected large sites, to the best modern standards, and with adequate time and financial resources. These sites, which would have to be chosen in the light of possibly conflicting factors of current development requirements and archaeological needs, will have to serve for all time as type-sites of London's archaeology. With this in mind the choice of sites should be influenced as much by their potential for demonstrating what was normal and typical in the evolution of the city, as by the likelihood that they might produce exceptional and remarkable situations or structures, perhaps inherently less informative about the general course of London's history. For the Anglo-Saxon and medieval periods, the evidence of the available written sources would be critical in the selection of sites. Such a selection would inevitably include a number of central sites likely to produce information about the origins and early Roman nucleus of London, as well as several sites along the waterfront where the archaeological deposits of all periods are relatively undisturbed and of particular importance (*5.9*).

(*b*) Excavations on a smaller scale designed to examine specific and limited problems. Such excavations might range from the cutting of sections through the defences or across individual streets, whenever possible in the course of some rearrangement, to the investigation of a whole structure such as a church. These excavations, although properly conducted archaeological operations, would be opportunist, unlike those in the first category where arrangements would deliberately be made to provide for large-scale archaeological work on the basis of archaeological rather than redevelopment needs.

(*c*) The systematic observation and recording of the archaeological evidence revealed in each and every disturbance of the ground throughout the City, and the collection of artefacts from these sites. The importance of this activity in establishing the extent of the occupied area at successive periods, both within the walls and in the suburbs, has been stressed in several places in this survey (*4.13, 15, 19, 29, 44* and *53*).

How soon must these problems be solved?

6.14   There are only two ways to reach some estimate of the time that is left during which enough of London's archaeology will survive to make further investigation of the main problems worthwhile. One is to examine the fate of individual areas; the other is to look at redevelopment trends in the City as a whole. The archeological deposits below London's pavements are a wasting stock: their total is finite and a great part has already been spent. The examples shown in *fig.7* and discussed in *5.8* and *5.9* are clear enough. Half the basilica-forum complex and half the so-called 'governor's palace' of Roman London have already gone, and at least another quarter of the forum has been partially destroyed. Since these are the only two major building complexes whose total extent is known, they are the only Roman examples which can be quoted in this way. Future developments planned in these areas are at present relatively slight, but the situation on the waterfront is quite the reverse. Here the effect is now being felt of a major trend in the City's recent history, the movement downstream of London's port activities (*5.11*). The result is that in an area where only about one-quarter of the archaeological deposits have been destroyed or damaged to date, development planned for the next five years and already in progress will destroy the archaeological potential of a further 39% of the Thames frontage (*5.9*). Two-thirds (63%) of the waterfront will have ceased to exist in archaeological terms by 1977. It takes little effort to see that if present trends are continued the whole frontage will have been redeveloped by 1983, ten years from now.

6.15   The general trends outlined in *5.11–17* with regard to the City as a whole reveal that the particular conditions affecting the redevelopment of the waterfront are being matched in the remainder of the City by other factors only slightly less pressing. At the most 190 acres (77 hectares) remain to be redeveloped out of the 441 acres (178 hectares) within street blocks. It seems probable that this may be achieved within the next fifteen years, by 1988.

6.16   Even before this redevelopment is completed a start will have been made on rebuilding the structures of the later forties, fifties, and sixties. Below some of these buildings archaeological deposits are known still to survive, usually in small pockets and heavily disturbed by foundation piles. From 1990 or so onwards archaeological activity in London will be restricted to mopping up these last pockets of evidence, and to an occasional operation in the 22 acres (9 hectares) of open space, below listed buildings or, where there is anything still left, below the streets.

6.17   Some indication of the likely course to be followed by redevelopment can be seen by comparing *Maps 7* and *8*, noting the areas of out-of-date commercial buildings that are probable candidates for early reconstruction. When *Map 8* is read over *Map 5* the way in which the developments of the next five years fill in the spaces between deeper constructions already existing is most striking. These visual comparisons appear to confirm the arguments from the figures quoted above and in *Chapter 5*.

6.18   Granted the uncertainty surrounding redevelopment in the light of changing economic forecasts, and given the inadequacy of the information about future projects available for this survey, the general conclusion is clear enough. There are at the very most twenty years left in which to discover the earlier history of our nation's capital. More probably only fifteen years remain. If immediate arrangements are not made to cope with this problem on an adequate scale, we shall simply never know how London changed from century to century and why and when the City took on its present pattern. The loss will be as serious as if all the early archives of the city had been carted away from Guildhall and burnt unread.

7 The future of London's past: outline of a solution

Objectives

7.1   Other historic cities in Britain, faced on a smaller scale with the problems now besetting the archaeology of London, have established research or excavation committees with professional archaeological units to deal with the situation on a full-time, long-term basis. Among such cities are Exeter, Lincoln, Norwich, Oxford, Southampton, Winchester, and York (*9*. Heighway 1972, paras 5.1–11).

7.2   The City of London does not possess such a unit although its archaeological problems, whether from the academic point of view or in relation to modern development, are more intractable both in kind and degree than those of any other city in this kingdom. The archaeological evidence for London's past will have ceased to exist by the later 1980s. It is, therefore, essential that an archaeological unit should be established in the City on a fully professional basis and within the shortest possible time.

7.3   The aim of such a unit would be to study the origin and subsequent development of the City, using appropriate means to ensure the thorough investigation and recording of archaeological evidence before its destruction by modern development.

7.4   A City of London Archaeological Unit would have the following interlocking tasks:

(*a*) The continuous evaluation of the archaeological situation in relation to development proposals.
(*b*) Long-term archaeological planning and liaison with all relevant Corporation, business, and development interests.
(*c*) The making of recommendations concerning the City's archaeology to the City of London Corporation, the Department of the Environment, and other relevant public bodies and private owners.
(*d*) The conduct of excavations on threatened and, where academically necessary, on unthreatened sites, and the observation and recording of archaeological information throughout the City.
(*e*) The documentary and archaeological research required for a proper evaluation and comprehension of the current archaeological situation and of the results and potential of past and future excavations.
(*f*) The publication of previous unpublished excavations in the City (as need be), and of all future excavations undertaken by the unit.

```
                          DIRECTOR
             |                              |
     (DEPUTY DIRECTOR)              (ASSISTANT DIRECTOR)

1. Excavation and   2. Finds handling,  3. Technical   4. Editorial and   5. Archive and   6. Administra-
   observation         storage, and        and            publication        historical       tion and
                       study               scientific                        research         liaison
```

Organization

7.5   If the establishment of a professional unit does provide the basis for a solution of London's archaeological problems – and there seems to be broad agreement from previous experience in other places that it does – there then arise detailed questions concerning the composition of the unit and its relationship to existing bodies. It will be convenient to look first at the requirements of the unit for permanent staff, voluntary help, and premises.

7.6   The tasks summarized in *7.4* and considered in detail in earlier paragraphs (e.g., *4.52, 6.6, 6.13*)

suggest that the unit will need to be active in the following areas:

(*a*) excavation and observation;
(*b*) handling, study, and storage of finds;
(*c*) technical and scientific support;
(*d*) editorial work for publication;
(*e*) the maintenance of an archaeological archive and the conduct of relevant historical research;
(*f*) its own administration, and regular liaison with Corporation departments and private interests.

The diagram above shows how these activities might be organized.

7.7   In such a scheme, where the total staff of the unit would be relatively small, the duties of the deputy and assistant director would probably fall upon the senior or most suitable person in one of the individual sections, so that the leader of the excavation and observation section, for example, might also act as deputy director of the whole unit. Such arrangements would depend on the abilities and qualities of the available personnel and the eventual size of the unit. The initial arrangements might well suggest such a combination of tasks. Later, the need for a separate post of deputy or assistant director, or both, might emerge. The intention of the proposed scheme is to ensure a proper division and control of the work in hand, with clearly defined areas of responsibility and a simple structure which will enable the director to concentrate on his two main tasks: the archaeological direction and academic control of the unit's activity and the top-level contacts with Corporation and development interests without which the unit could not function. The professional and academic ability required of the director of a City of London Archaeological Unit, combined as they must be with administrative experience, an understanding of the working of local government and of business, and with skill and persistence in negotiation, demand a senior appointment at a salary equivalent to that of a university professor.

7.8   The composition of the six sections shown in the diagram in *7.6* must be outlined. The requirements set out in *6.13* suggest that the *Excavation and Observation Section* should be able to carry out at least one major excavation and several smaller excavations simultaneously, while at the same time maintaining constant observation and record of construction sites where archaeological levels are being disturbed. This work will require at least three site supervisors at the AP 4/5 level of the local government salary scale, one of whom would be responsible for the skilled and arduous task of observing construction sites (*3.15*), and not less than five assistant supervisors at the AP 2/3 level. It seems inescapable that there should also be a separate team concerned solely with the waterfront, where there is an urgent need to undertake long-term excavations on sites where waterlogged conditions will have preserved an extensive range of organic material requiring specialized techniques of excavation, record, handling, and study. The waterfront team will require a site supervisor at AP 4/5, and a minimum of three assistant supervisors at AP 2/3. The *Excavation and Observation Section* will thus require a total of four site supervisors at the AP 4/5 level, and eight assistant supervisors at AP 2/3. This is the minimum staff given the number of sites subject to redevelopment plans at any one moment, and the limited time available. Furthermore, site supervisors will have to prepare their share of the reports for publication as far as possible on the completion of each site, and although the other sections of the unit are designed to facilitate this process, this requirement will mean that the unit will rarely have all four site supervisors simultaneously engaged on excavations. The section will need at least thirty experienced site-workers or diggers on the AP1 scale, and will require a section head, who may also act as deputy director of the unit (see *7.7*), at the SO 1/2 level. A possible scheme for this section would be as follows:

Excavation and Observation Section

SECTION HEAD
(perhaps also Deputy Director of the unit)
SO 1/2

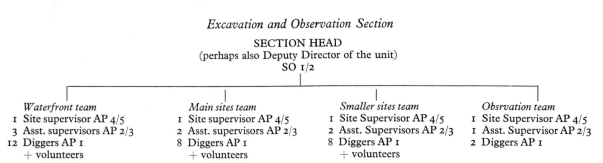

Waterfront team	*Main sites team*	*Smaller sites team*	*Obsrvation team*
1 Site supervisor AP 4/5	1 Site supervisor AP 4/5	1 Site Supervisor AP 4/5	1 Site Supervisor AP 4/5
3 Asst. supervisors AP 2/3	2 Asst. supervisors AP 2/3	2 Asst. Supervisors AP 2/3	1 Asst. Supervisor AP 2/3
12 Diggers AP 1	8 Diggers AP 1	8 Diggers AP 1	2 Diggers AP 1
+ volunteers	+ volunteers	+ volunteers	

The staff of the first three teams may seem large at first sight, but is designed to include the site planner(s), and to be able to cope with a labour-force considerably augmented by volunteers (*7.12*). Both the waterfront and smaller sites team will need to be able to split into sections to undertake several excavations at the same time: hence the need for sufficient supervisory personnel.

7.9   An essential part of any excavation is the handling of the movable finds. Experience suggests that the expertise developed in dealing with the processing of finds during an excavation can be profitably applied to the subsequent problems of storage, production, and study, the latter especially in regard to the bulk materials, such as pottery. A permanent unit can take advantage of this situation in a way which was not possible when excavations were undertaken by temporary *ad hoc* teams. For the London unit it may seem appropriate that the finds system proposed for *Section 2* should be controlled by a finds supervisor at the AP 4/5 level. Such a person would be responsible for organizing the processing of the finds of each field team during the course of excavations, as well as for subsequent storage, for the distribution of individual classes needing specialists' reports, and for the study, in conjunction with the site supervisors, of those materials, especially pottery, which would be undertaken by the unit's own staff. To carry out these tasks the finds supervisor would need finds teams to operate constantly with each of the field teams, as well as a base team for sorting, distribution, and study, and a storekeeper. The appropriate staff would probably be four finds assistants at AP 2/3, supported by five finds workers at AP 1, and a storekeeper at Technical Grade 2. If the ratio of a finds staff totalling eleven, to an excavation section totalling forty-two seems high, it must be remembered that the finds are likely to be very great in quantity, that the finds section will be deeply involved in their study for publication, as well as in their day-to-day handling, and that the permanent labour-force of the excavation is likely to be considerably augmented by volunteers (7.12), thus greatly increasing the volume of material. It cannot be too strongly emphasized that it is the sheer bulk of finds from urban excavations which controls the production of final reports. Unless the finds organization is adequately staffed, an ever-increasing backlog of unsorted material will threaten the academic viability of the whole project. It should perhaps be added that the proposed finds organization, even in its storage facility, would not in any way seek to duplicate the functions of a museum. It is designed solely to handle a very large quantity of material during the course of a progression from excavation to publication. It will be an important part of the finds section's activity to arrange with the relevant museum for the regular transfer of finds (subject to their owners' agreement), once the processes required for publication have been completed.

7.10   It seems appropriate that the unit's technical and scientific services should be grouped together in a single section, *Section 3*. This would include a conservation laboratory, a small environmental laboratory, a photographic facility, and a survey and drawing office. The head of this section, responsible to the director via the deputy director for all the technical and scientific services required by the unit, might be the most senior officer of the section for the time being. In proposing that the unit should have a conservation laboratory there is no intention of restricting the conservation activities of any museum that might be the ultimate recipient of the finds, but only of ensuring that the conservation necessary to ensure the stability of the finds and their study and drawing for publication can be undertaken by the unit as expeditiously as possible, and in a work-flow adapted to the unit's own needs rather

than the requirements of another body. A conservator at the AP 4/5 level with a trainee at AP 1/2 would seem appropriate. The environmental study of London's past is a field of inquiry that has scarcely yet been developed. The main need is for the unit to have the services of an environmental archaeologist who will be able to ensure that the opportunities for environmental research are grasped, who will be able to direct the unit's sampling policy and organize the collaboration of outside specialists in the many disciplines concerned, and who will be qualified to correlate the resulting reports for the final publications. Such an environmental archaeologist, who might well have been trained at the Institute of Archaeology of the University of London, would himself probably be fully qualified only in a limited field, such as soil science or botany. In this field he would undertake the unit's work himself; in other fields he would play the correlating role. The environmental archaeologist would probably be at the AP 4/5 level, possibly with a technician at Technical Grade 1/2. The unit will also require a photographer at Technical Grade 4/5, perhaps with an assistant at Technical 1/2, two draughtsmen for publication drawings, one for finds and the other for plans and sections (a division of work that need not be rigidly adhered to) at Technical Grade 2/3, and a surveyor at AP 2/3. The latter post would be for large-scale survey work and the architectural recording of major structures: the usual archaeological planning, like the drawing of sections, would be the responsibility of the individual field teams of the excavation section (7.8).

7.11   The three sections which it was suggested in 7.6 might fall to the responsibility of the assistant director of the unit can be more simply outlined. *Section 4*, editorial and publication, will need an editor at AP 4/5, an editorial assistant at AP 2/3, and a typist at Clerical 1. *Section 5*, handling the archaeological archive of the unit and undertaking the necessary historical research, will need a historian, who would probably take charge of the section, at AP 4/5, an archaeological 'archivist' at AP 2/3, and a typist at Clerical 1. *Section 6* will handle the unit's administration and the vitally important task of regular liaison at administrative level with Corporation and private interests. It seems possible that the unit's administrator could be responsible for both these tasks, and could suitably act as assistant director, with general responsibility also for Sections 4 and 5. This grouping of responsibilities would allow the assistant director to prepare for the director continuous evaluations of the archaeological potential of proposed developments, drawing on the records of Section 5 and the liaison information coming into Section 6. Since this evaluation will be an essential part of the unit's forward planning, and will require a sound archaeological appreciation, the proposed grouping of responsibilities suggests that the unit's administrator, if also serving as assistant director, must be a professional archaeologist rather than a non-specialist. This appointment would probably be at AP 5, and would be supported by three clerical officers, one at Clerical Grade 3, one at Senior Scale A, and the other at Clerical 1, who would also supply secretarial services to the director and deputy director, and typing as required for the rest of the unit. If arrangements can be made for the finances of the unit to be handled by an established finance department (see *7.15*), this will lighten the burden on the administrator. If such an arrangement were not possible, a financial officer would have to be added to the unit's staff.

7.12   The suggestions for a City of London Archaeological Unit outlined in *7.6–11* provide the basis for a professional operation designed to operate effectively in conditions of administrative complexity and considerable urgency. It is essential that this organization should be strengthened by the great fund of volunteer effort which has played so notable a part in London's archaeology in recent years. The establishment of a professional unit of this kind should be seen not as restricting the opportunity for amateur involvement, but as opening up even wider avenues for amateur participation at almost all levels. It must be obvious from what has been said in *7.8* and *7.9* that considerable extra help will be needed both on the excavations themselves, and in the backroom work on the finds. If the experience of the Winchester Research Unit provides a parallel, opportunities for amateur involvement under professional guidance will exist also in the more specialized work, technical, scientific, and historical, of Sections 3 and 5. It will be a prime duty of any future London unit to encourage and take full advantage of all the opportunities that exist to intensify its work and increase its output through amateur participation. Only in this way will the very considerable financial expenditure involved in the creation of such a unit be put to its maximum effective use. In addition to volunteers available locally from the London region, the unit would need to make use of the student volunteer labour available during university vacations, and especially during the summer months. The rates of subsistence paid to such volunteers are currently being adjusted, but £1·50 a day seems likely to be the scale adopted for those having to live away from home to attend the excavations. From this sum appropriate deductions would have to be made for food and lodging if the unit were to operate the normal kind of hostel system. This rate of subsistence should be regarded as the maximum. Student volunteers, particularly from overseas, are frequently prepared to attend excavations of this scale and importance in return for board and lodging alone, without receiving subsistence, and in view of the saving this represents and the benefit the volunteer receives from the training and experience provided, this tendency should certainly be encouraged. If necessary, additional short-term supervisors and assistant supervisors could probably be engaged under the same arrangements with the addition of some weekly or fee payment. The unit should probably be prepared to operate with a student volunteer force of up to 150 individuals for a period of at least ten weeks each summer.

7.13   The expectation of considerable student volunteer and amateur – or perhaps better said, part-time – participation in the work of a future unit will have some reflection in any estimate of the unit's requirements for accommodation. Of the proposed permanent staff of seventy-four, at least half will be constantly in the field. A minimum of 4,000 sq. feet of space will be needed, at least one-third of it for handling and storing finds. It seems probable that it will not be possible to find all this in one place, or on a permanent basis. It should also be stressed that the space required could probably be adapted in buildings which would not be acceptable for normal office accommodation, and indeed that a warehouse building, some of it suitably partitioned and modified, might be ideal.

7.14   It remains in this discussion of organization to consider the relationship of the proposed unit to existing bodies. To some extent this will turn on the question of whether the unit should deal with the archaeology of the administrative area of the City and County of the City of London alone, or whether it should be part of a larger unit concerned with the archaeology of Greater London, including the City of Westminster and all the other London boroughs. There is archaeological sense in both views: on the one hand a unit charged with the principal archaeological objective, the City itself with the greater part of its ancient suburbs, the area in which an immediate and especially intensive effort is required; on the other, the possibility of one organization able to comprehend the interlocking archaeology of the City and its hinterland. Even if, however, the larger proposal were to be adopted, the archaeology of the City forms a separate problem, whether of rescue work or research, so that a Greater London unit would have to include a separate operational section for the City, to all intents and purposes identical to the unit proposed in these pages. The importance of the City's archaeology is indeed of a quite different order from that of the surrounding area: whatever position is finally reached, this fact must be given full weight and safeguards established to ensure that the effort in the City is not diluted by the pressure of other equally urgent but historically less vital tasks. On balance it seems probable that the great difficulties and particular importance of the City's archaeology should be reflected in the creation of a separate City of London unit.

7.15 If this were to be the case, there appear to be three possible solutions: the proposed unit might be set up as a department or sub-department of the City Corporation; it might form part of the new Museum of London; or it might be an independent body with its own governing committee and charitable status. In various forms all three solutions are at present in satisfactory operation in historic towns throughout the country. This survey is not the place in which the issue can be argued out, let alone settled. Some points may, however, be worth making. It will be greatly to the unit's advantage if its finances could be administered by an already existing finance department. This would happen in the normal course of events if the unit were a part of the City Corporation or of the Museum of London; it is a service which could be provided by either body, or any other appropriate organization, if the unit were independent. Thus the University of York handles the finances of the independent York Archaeological Trust; the City of Winchester handles those of the independent Winchester Research Unit. The bulk of the proposed London unit's finances will presumably come from the Department of the Environment and the City of London Corporation, and this will rightly give both bodies a large say in the running of the unit. The unit may, however, be most effective in arguing its case among many competing interests if it is detached from both these great concerns and is either independent or attached to the Musem of London, itself an independent body. If the latter solution were adopted, it is clear that the unit should be, as it were, in parallel with the museum side, the unit director enjoying direct access to the Board of Governors. Such would also be the case if the unit were to be established under the City Corporation, where the director would certainly require direct access to the Library Committee, if that were in fact the appropriate body. This discussion may, however, be overtaken by the events now moving rapidly within the Department of the Environment towards the establishment of a series of independent regional archaeological units covering the whole country. If this comes about, it is important that the London unit should form part of the national organization, within which there will be appropriate machinery for the evolution of national research policy, as well as for more day-to-day procedures such as the agreement of salary scales and conditions of service. The independent archaeological committee and the independent unit already enjoy a highly successful record in other cities. The independent unit may also be the proper solution for London's past.

Costs

7.16 The cost of the establishment proposed in *7.6–11* in a full year is shown in Table VII. Salaries are normally quoted at the lowest point on the national salary scales in use by local authorities 1972–3, and conform to the suggestions now being made by the Department of the Environment for the employment of archaeological staff in rescue units. London weighting is *not* included. To the basic cost of the salaries must be added the cost of employer's superannuation contributions, and further sums for Equal Annual Charge, National Insurance, and Graduated Pensions, a total of perhaps £20,294. The establishment cost of the unit in a full year might therefore be:

	£
Salaries	109,273
Additional charges	20,294
	£129,567

7.17 Experience with other archaeological units suggests that the running costs, including the rent of premises, and the purchase of supplies, might amount to one-fifth of the establishment costs, in this case to (£129,567÷5) or £25,913. In London this figure would have to be sufficient to cover the high rents that would probably be necessary (by comparison with the rest of the country), even for property of the kind envisaged in *7.13*. It should also contain an element (perhaps as much as £2,000) for the payment of fees for, e.g. radio-carbon dating and other specialist services. To this basic figure for running costs should be added further sums for transport, plant-hire, and publications. The unit at full strength might need as many as six vehicles. If purchased for about £1,200 each, with their cost spread over five years, and with running charges at about £400 a vehicle each year, the cost would be about £3,840 in a year. The use of plant will be an important feature of the unit's activity, for bulk excavation of disturbed or relatively unimportant deposits, for soil-handling after manual excavation, for dump control, and for the removal of soil from sites of restricted area. A sum of perhaps £5,000 may not be unrealistic in a full year. Finally, with the cost of printing and publishing now at exceptional levels, it may be wise for the unit to build up a sinking fund from which subsidies in support of its publications might be drawn. The annual costs of the unit other than salaries might therefore be as follows:

	£
Basic running costs	25,913
Transport	3,840
Plant-hire	5,000
Publications sinking fund	2,500
	37,253

Table VII

City of London Archaeological Unit: proposed establishment

Post	Scale	Salary £	Number	Basic cost £
Director	University professor	5,500	1	5,500
Deputy director	SO 1/2	2,994	1	2,994
Assistant director	AP 5	2,388	1	2,388
Site supervisors, finds supervisors, conservator, environmental archaeologist, editor, and historian	AP 4/5	2,100	9	18,900
Assistant supervisors, finds assistants, surveyor, editorial assistant, and archivist	AP 2/3	1,530	15	22,950
Site and finds workers, trainee conservator	AP 1	1,251	36	45,036
Photographer	Technical 4/5	1,530	1	1,530
Draughtsmen, storekeeper	Technical 2/3	1,143	3	3,429
Photographic assistant, environmental technician	Technical 1/2	987*	2	1,974
Clerical officer	Clerical 3	1,530	1	1,530
Secretary	Senior scale A	1,251	1	1,251
Typists	Clerical 1	597	3	1,791
Totals	—	—	74	109,273

*At half-way point on scale.

7.18   In addition to local volunteers, for whom a subsistence rate of 75p a day has been proposed nationally, to cover fares and lunch, the unit should be able to use the services of up to 150 student volunteers during a period, or periods, totalling ten weeks each year (7.12). At the rate of £1·50 a day proposed for volunteers staying away from home to take part in the work, and accepting that the payments are made for seven days each week, this would cost the unit an additional £15,750. These outline estimates do not include the cost to the unit of running hostel accommodation and providing meals for these volunteers, for with the rate at £1·50 a day it should be possible to make realistic deductions to cover these costs. The additional cost of subsistence payments to local volunteers is also excluded, as it is impossible to estimate, and can be adjusted in the first instance against the sum envisaged for student volunteers coming from a distance.

7.19   The addition of 150 student volunteers to the permanent digging force of thirty, providing a work-force of 180 in (essentially) the summer months, will overtax the twelve permanent site and assistant supervisors in the Excavation and Observation Section. Additional supervisors will, there-

fore, be needed on a temporary basis, as has been normal practice for years in British archaeology. If ten additional supervisors are provided at a rate (including subsistence) of £4 a day, seven days a week, the cost to the unit for a ten-week season would be £2,800. During this period the ratio of supervisors to diggers would then be 22:180, or about one supervisor to eight workers, a ratio that has been found effective elsewhere. If these figures are adopted, the cost to the unit of student volunteers each year will be:

	£
Volunteer diggers	15,750
Temporary supervisors	2,800
	£18,550

7.20   The figures put forward in the previous paragraphs show that the cost of the proposed City of London Archaeological Unit in a full year might be:

	£
Establishment (7.16)	129,567
Running costs, etc. (7.17)	37,253
Volunteer labour (7.18) 19)	18,550
	£185,370

This is a large sum, but it is the result of a careful analysis of the tasks that need to be done. Furthermore, it is not out of scale with experience in other cities. In 1971–2, which included the 1971 excavation season, the cost of the Winchester excavations and unit came to £42,000 in a city less than half the area of walled London, and far less severely threatened by development. This figure relates to a year early in the recent period of monetary inflation. The revised budget for the York Archaeological Trust in its second year, 1973–4, is £90,000 and the operation has by no means reached its final scale. The figures for a London unit set out above relate to a year at full staff. They would not be reached until the second year of operation at the earliest, and it would be more likely the third year before the unit was at full strength.

7.21   It would not be useful to attempt here to forecast the actual expenditure of a City of London Archaeological Unit year by year. Quite apart from the normal progression of staff up the incremental ladder (the cost of which would be offset to some extent in time by replacement at lower levels), there are obvious uncertainties about the future rate of inflation, and the revisions in salary scales that may arise as a result, as well as about the time that will be needed to bring the unit to its full complement. Any savings on this latter count will be partly offset in the first year by the expenditure needed for the initial equipment of the unit, for the conversion of premises, and for the other charges necessarily incurred in setting up a new organization. Fortunately, at least in financial terms, the formation of a City Archaeological Unit does not imply an open-ended commitment. If the views put forward in *Chapter 6* are right, there are at the most twenty years left in which such a unit can serve a useful function. After that time its raw material, the archaeological deposits of the City's past, will for all practical purposes no longer exist. There is little to be gained by trying to be more precise. The figures suggest the general order of expenditure required to investigate and record the archaeology of the City while there is still time: £185,000 odd in a full year, and something of the order of £2 million during the next ten years.

7.22   What might be the sources of finance for expenditure at this level? It is worth first to try and see the suggested annual sum in the context of the City Corporation's expenses funded by the General Rate. The recent revaluation of properties for rating purposes has given the City a rateable value of £242,804,926. The estimated product of a new penny rate is £2,285,000 in 1973–4, and expenditure of £185,000 on an archaeological unit would therefore be equivalent to a rate of 0·08p, or differently expressed, would be 8·1% of the estimated product of a new penny rate. There is no reason to suppose,

however, that the City would be asked to foot the entire bill for an archaeological unit, however large or small. The Department of the Environment's contribution to archaeology in the City has always been notable (*3.14,19*), and in the current debate over regional archaeological units a fairly clear indication has emerged that the Department would expect to carry about half the cost, provided that the relevant local authority or authorities made themselves responsible for the remainder and especially for all or a substantial part of the cost of the salaries of permanent staff. There would clearly have to be considerable discussion to achieve a balanced sharing of the costs of a City unit, which cannot indeed be directly compared with one of the proposed regional units. Even so, it seems not unreasonable to suppose that the cost could be fairly equally shared between the Corporation and the Department, each contributing something over £93,000 in a full year. On the City's side this would be equivalent to a rate of 0·04p or 4·1% of the estimated product of a new penny rate in 1973–4.

7.23   It has sometimes been argued that the cost of rescue excavations should be made a charge on the developers, 'on the grounds that if cultural levels are to be destroyed, the agents of that destruction should contribute to repairing its consequences' (*9.* Heighway 1972, para. 7.11). This is the procedure in some Continental countries, and could well have a general application in Britain. Yet it may not be entirely relevant in the City of London, where the domestic rate-payer contributes a very small proportion of the rate product, and where the great companies, for whom developments are undertaken and by whom they are intitiated, carry by far the greater part of the rate burden. It makes, in the end, very little difference to archaeology whether the work is financed by the individual firms involved in any given development or by the Corporation and the Department of the Environment, but the second solution may not only be simpler and more likely to happen, it may also be much fairer to the firms concerned. The main reason why so much archaeology must be done in the next ten to twenty years is that so little was done in the last thirty years. It seems proper, therefore, that the cost of this work should be evenly spread through rates and taxes, rather than that it should fall on the limited number of firms who happen to be developing now and in the future.

The law

7.24   Given that the problems of London's archaeology can be analysed and a solution proposed; granted that the money can be found and a unit established; this may still be no insurance that the work can be done. Is it possible to overcome the developer's fears that his projects will be delayed, to allay his doubts about the value of archaeology and the professional status of archaeologists? Even with goodwill and mutual comprehension, is it possible to build a period for archaeological investigation into a tight construction schedule? The problems faced by archaeologists working in towns have been surveyed on a national scale by the Council for British Archaeology in their recent report *The Erosion of History: Archaeology and Planning in Towns* (9. Heighway 1972). Sections 4 and 7 of that report, the latter presenting the recommendations resulting from the survey, form the basis of what follows here.

7.25 Any non-specialist seeking to discover the importance of archaeological factors in relation to what may seem the more immediate and pressing problems of modern urban life might well begin by asking what steps society has taken to ensure the safeguarding of archaeological remains, or at least of the information they can be made to yield. This country has indeed a long tradition of care for the visible remains of its past. Unfortunately *The Erosion of History* was forced to conclude that existing 'Ancient Monuments legislation is not an effective protection for the buried remains of the urban past' (9. Heighway 1972, para. 4.1). Very few urban sites have in fact been scheduled under the Ancient Monuments Acts, even where the exact location of a structure of the first importance is well known. It is only during the last year, for example, that steps have been taken to schedule the site of the Roman forum and basilica in London and thus to provide these already eroded sites with the minimal protection which scheduling affords (*4.13*). Scheduling, even if it were carried out on a much larger scale, is not the answer to the problems of urban archaeology where sites can rarely be preserved intact and where the fundamental problem is to ensure their investigation and record before more or less inevitable destruction. Scheduling is, by its very nature, concerned with individual sites and monuments. By contrast, what is necessary in towns is to secure some recognition that the whole ancient area is an archaeological artefact and that prior thought should be given before any part of it is disturbed or destroyed.

7.26 The factor which has to be grasped is the archaeological potential of any given development; that is to say, the likely value in archaeological and historical terms of the information which might come from an investigation of the site – or which might be lost if the site were destroyed without record. Thus the most important single recommendation of *The Erosion of History* was 'to secure by law that the archaeological potential of any proposed development should be considered when planning permission is granted' (9. Heighway 1972, para. 7.3).

It will be noticed that the consideration would be mandatory, but that nothing is said at this stage of mandatory investigation. Experience has often shown that recognition of the archaeological problem is sufficient to ensure that suitable arrangements can be made to deal with it. Subsequent paragraphs (*7.29* and *30–1*) will discuss the legislation which seems to be required to cope with more difficult cases.

7.27 If the archaeological potential of any given site is to be reliably estimated, it can obviously only be done by a professional evaluation of all the factors involved. The first requirement is an archaeological town survey or map against which, as it were, can be read off the archaeological implications of a proposed development. Other factors are involved, such as the extent of existing destruction and survival of the deposits, the nature of the deposits themselves, and their potential contribution to existing knowledge. This present survey provides in *Maps 1–8* and in *Appendix I* the means to make an outline assessment of the archaeological potential of any given site in the City, and includes a detailed listing of the archaeological potential of sites to be developed over the next five years. A detailed assessment of each site will also be needed, and this would be one of the tasks of a City Archaeological Unit (*7.4a*).

7.28 Consideration of the archaeological potential of a site is useful to everyone concerned. Its value to the archaeologist is clear enough: he has some idea what to expect and he is in a position to decide what he can try to do. The developer also benefits. Opposition to archaeological work is rarely based on a conviction that it is unimportant; it usually results from fear of delay and financial loss. In fact archaeologists have rarely caused delays, if only because they have no legal powers for doing so. Stories of the loss caused by discovery of the Mithras temple, all exaggerated, have done great harm to relations between archaeologists and the development and construction industry as a whole (*3.17*): indeed, if archaeologists had the ability to delay work sometimes attributed to them, there would never have been any need for this survey of London's past, or rather of its unrecorded disappearance. The value to a developer of knowing the archaeological potential of a site long before he has made his plans, before indeed he has obtained planning permission, is that he then knows what to expect. It is at this stage that negotiations should take place between archaeologists and developers, and at this stage that arrangements could be made to phase archaeological work into the development programme. The corollary to this must be that the developer who had co-operated throughout and then found himself subject to delay from an unexpected discovery (and such will still sometimes occur however detailed the survey of archaeological potential), would have to be compensated for any loss. It will thus be incumbent on archaeologists to make realistic appraisals and stick rigidly to agreed schedules, and this, having always had to work with limited resources, they have already learnt do do.

7.29   It is obvious that a City Archaeological Unit will want to work closely with developers, so as to be able to provide surveys of archaeological potential early in a project. Some of this work would be confidential and this is possibly another argument for a relatively independent status for the unit. Even with the possibility of such relationships, however, there may still be cases where arrangements cannot be made with the developer. *The Erosion of History* recommended, therefore, that legislation should be brought forward to ensure 'that an archaeologically accedited person should be given access to building sites with archaeological deposits and objects' for the purpose of observation and record while work was in progress (9. Heighway 1972, para. 7.5, cf. para. 4.9). This suggestion is in line with the recommendations of the Walsh Committee on Field Monuments (Cmnd. 3904), para.145.

7.30   Observation and record during contract works should, in all normal cases, be easily arranged between the archaeologist and the developer. No delays are involved and with good relations and good sense there need be no difficulties. Observations of this kind are very important, and a City unit would be heavily committed in ensuring that they were thoroughly maintained (*3.15, 6.13c, 7.8*). Nevertheless such observations – watching briefs, as they are sometimes called – are a second best and are never any substitute for controlled excavation. Excavation, however, takes time and it is here that fears of delay arise. Once again, part of the solution lies in consideration of the archaeological potential of the proposed development at the earliest possible stage. If the site is lying open there should be no difficulty in planning an excavation to take place and be completed before the start of contract works. At Baynard Castle, for example, the site lay open for at least two years before contract works began and during this time major excavations could have been undertaken. If, however, a site is occupied by buildings in use, which are only to be demolished when new works are due to begin, the problems are much more serious. Even here the consideration of the archaeological factor at the earliest possible date may allow the demolition programme to be brought forward, so that an excavation can still be completed before the proposed start of contract works. Such a solution would cause a smaller loss of rent on the old building, than if the completion of the new structure were delayed. This problem will not arise if the

standing building is out of use, in which case it should be possible to advance its demolition without undue difficulty. Excavation in the cellars, prior to demolition, may also prove possible, as recently in Bush Lane House. But the limitations are such that a cleared site is nearly always preferable.

7.31   There will still be cases, however, where the owner may refuse to permit excavation. For this reason *The Erosion of History* recommended 'that there should be provision in law to secure time for excavation if required' (9. Heighway 1972, para 7.6, cf. para. 4.10). This recommendation is also in line with the proposals of the Walsh Committee referred to above, and the Secretary of State for the Environment has indicated in the House of Commons that he intends bringing forward legislation to this effect (*Hansard, 19, April 1972, Written Answers, col. 96*). It is very much to be hoped that such powers will only be needed as a long-stop. They would be based on the view that the evidence of the past is a common possession of all our people and that it should not be destroyed unheeded for either private profit or public convenience. This is the rationale behind the rapidly growing involvement of the Government in rescue archaeology. It must lead also to a final conclusion, that compensation should not be payable for delays or increased expenditure resulting from the archaeological investigation of a development site, unless they were unforeseen when planning permission was granted. In other words, that the reasonable and foreseeable implications of archaeological investigation should be regarded as part of the job of preparing the way for any new development which will cause the destruction of archaeological deposits. Although it is possible to argue further from this to the proposition that the developer should actually pay for, or at least contribute substantially to, the cost of rescue excavation and its subsequent publication, the City of London may be a case where this burden would be more fairly spread through rates and taxes (*7.23*).

7.32   Developers themselves have been heard to say in recent months that they would welcome legislation regarding archaeology since they would then know where they stood. Good legislation should reduce their concern that archaeology will cause them delay and considerable expense, and will keep to a minimum the delay and expense that may sometimes be involved. At present the situation is unsatisfactory for both sides, but if there is one thing certain, it is that a great deal can be achieved by goodwill and good professional relationships, and especially by a growing understanding of the nature and purpose of archaeology and of the seriousness and reliability of archaeologists. There are many success stories in rescue archaeology, and there is no reason to suppose that London need be different, even if the pressures there are of an order greater than elsewhere in the country. With the setting up of a City of London Archaeological Unit, and with surveys of archaeological potential at an early stage in planning, the problems that may arise can be taken into consideration on a sensible basis by all concerned, at the earliest possible date.

8 Conclusions

8.1   The City of London has been continuously occupied for nearly two thousand years. Below its present streets and buildings it is an archaeological artefact of great size and extreme complexity, an artefact which for a period of over a thousand years is the principal and often the only source of information about the origins and early history of the City. For a century and a half these buried remains of a distant and distinguished past have been investigated and recorded by a band of devoted antiquaries and scholars who salvaged what they could in conditions of unrelieved difficulty. Despite their efforts our knowledge of the archaeology of London is unsatisfactory in almost every respect. There has been neither the finance, nor the administration, neither the staff nor indeed always the will, to ensure that the remains of the past threatened by the needs of the present were investigated, recorded, and published for scholars and the general interest alike.

8.2   The emphasis of archaeological work in the City has been heavily concentrated on the Roman period. Even so, knowledge of the Roman city is far from adequate, while understanding of the archaeology of the Anglo-Saxon and later periods is minimal. Over about one-quarter of the City the archaeological deposits have already been totally destroyed; over a further three-fifths they have been at least partially damaged, usually with loss of the later deposits. The archaeology of the City is still reasonably intact over less than one-fifth of its area. The destruction varies in intensity from place to place. In certain areas, such as the top of the eastern hill around Cornhill where Roman London began, the destruction is already so extensive that few opportunities remain for archaeological work: these few must be fully exploited. Elsewhere, in the peripheral areas close to and beyond the City wall, for example, and especially along the waterfront, there has been less destruction of the buried layers, and correspondingly greater possibilities to undertake archaeological investigations still exist.

8.3   Unfortunately this situation will not long remain. Within about ten years the archaeological deposits along the waterfront will have been destroyed. Within fifteen years, or twenty at the most, the other areas of the City still undeveloped since 1945 will have been renewed. By the end of the 1980s the archaeology of the City will survive only in a few isolated pockets: below some open spaces, below a few churches, beneath some buildings in the conservation areas. The surviving areas of archaeological deposits will be entirely insufficient to preserve an adequate picture of the City's origin and development.

8.4   The major problems facing the archaeologist and historian can, however, probably be solved during the next ten to twenty years if steps are taken at once to set up an organization specifically charged to investigate and record the remaining archaeological evidence before its destruction by future development. Such an organization, a City of London Archaeological Unit, would have many tasks, but its principal activities would be the conduct of excavations, the observation of building sites, the study and publication of its results. Faced with a very large task, and one that must be achieved under the constant pressure of external but overriding factors, such a unit will need an adequate professional staff, a permanent base, and the support of volunteer workers, both local and coming from afar.

8.5   The cost of a City Archaeological Unit, properly staffed and equipped, will be high. In a full year expenditure may rise to £185,000, and the cost over the next ten years might reach £2 million. Previous experience in London and throughout the country suggests that at least half this expenditure might be carried by central Government funds through the Department of the Environment. The balance in such an arrangement would be the responsibility of the City Corporation. On an approximate initial estimate of £185,000 for a full year, the City contribution might thus be about £93,000, a sum equivalent to a rate of 0·04p in terms of the estimated product of a new penny rate for 1973-4.

8.6   A City Archaeological Unit, funded from at least two sources, would seem best organized either as a division of the new Museum of London, itself an independent body with a Board of Governors, or as an independent organization with its own governing committee and charitable status. The latter solution may be most appropriate in view of the course likely to be followed in the country as a whole for the regionalization of rescue archaeology, but the former solution, in which the Museum of London would play a role comparable to the landesmuseums of the Continent, has many attractive aspects.

8.7   There is very little time left: if the unit is to be successful it will need to work with development and business interests in the City in an atmosphere of goodwill, mutual confidence, and mutual comprehension. Part of the background to such a situa-tion would be good archaeological legislation which would protect and clarify the interests and res-ponsibilities of both sides. Archaeologists need to be able to evaluate development proposals in terms of the archaeological potential of the sites; they need access for observation and recording; they need time for excavation. Developers need security against unforseen and unwarranted delay, and consequent expenditure; they must be persuaded of the need for archaeological work, and they need to be sure of the professional competence of the archaeologists with whom they deal. Good law, good public rela-tions, and mutual understanding: all three are re-quired to ensure that this final attempt to learn of the origins and to understand the development of our nation's capital is attended by success.

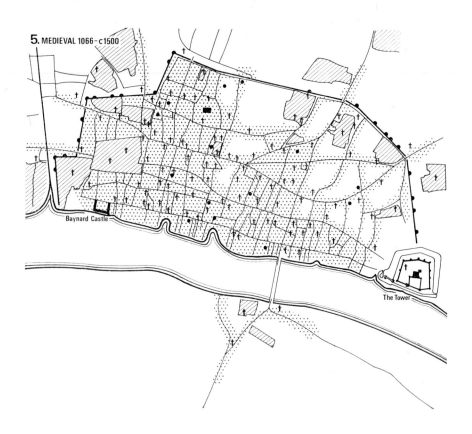

5. MEDIEVAL 1066–c1500

Baynard Castle

The Tower

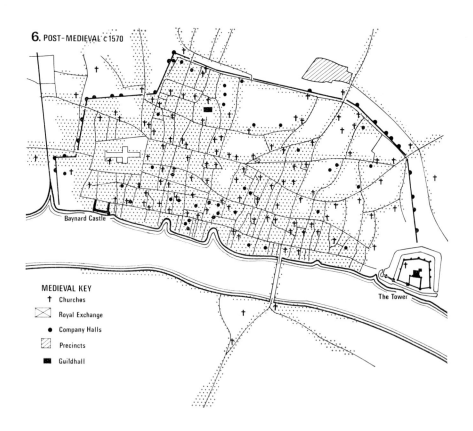

6. POST–MEDIEVAL c1570

Baynard Castle

The Tower

MEDIEVAL KEY

- † Churches
- ⊠ Royal Exchange
- ● Company Halls
- ▨ Precincts
- ▪ Guildhall

s, but in the case of
utions. (1 : 20,000)

Appendix I: Schedule

Sites to be developed in the City of London in the immediate future or within the next five years

The schedule attempts to show the archaeological potential of sites for which there is evidence of development proposals in the immediate future or within the next five years. The position is constantly changing, and existing proposals may be modified. The schedule shows the situation at 30 September 1972. Subsequent proposals may easily be dealt with in the same manner. It should be emphasized that the use of columns (6)–(8), allowing an estimate to be made of the depth of archaeological deposits remaining, is not intended to supersede site inspection, but only to give an idea of the probable situation.

Column (1) The reference numbers correspond to those shown on Map 8.

Column (2) The sites are listed within the 500 m. squares of the National Grid. Where sites overlap neighbouring squares, an entry will be found under both, and the overlap is indicated in column (2).

Column (3) Where a large site is being redeveloped the address given may not correspond completely with the site shown on Map 8. The mapped area is based where possible on site plans attached to the planning application.

Column (4) Outline planning permissions are indicated by the letter O (e.g., 13.1.72 O). Conditional permissions are indicated by C (e.g., 11.6.64 C). Schemes for which an Office Development Permit has been obtained, but which have not yet received planning permission, are indicated by ODP and the date (e.g., ODP 15.3.71).

Column (5) Proposed development or other comments about the area shown.

Columns (6) and (7) Height above OD is shown in metres. The Roman land surface is based on information shown on Map 6.

Column (8) Information based on Map 5. Three intensities of destruction of the archaeological levels are indicated:
T – TOTAL DESTRUCTION, tall buildings with two or more basements.
P – PARTIAL DESTRUCTION, tall buildings with one basement.
L – LIMITED DESTRUCTION, deposits probably cut into, but the deeper layers less disturbed.
Letters in brackets (e.g., (T)) indicate sites where the destroyed area does not extend over the whole of the site.

Columns (9), (10) and (11). Entries in square brackets [] indicate that the archaeological levels have probably already been totally or very extensively destroyed. In some of these cases there are already records of finds and/or observations on the site. Entries in round brackets ( ) indicate sites where little archaeological potential may be left, but which may warrant inspection in case, for example, part of the site may have been less disturbed.

(1) Ref. no.	(2) Other 500 m squares	(3) Address of site	(4) Date of planning permission	(5) Proposed development	(6) Approx. present land surface	(7) Approx. Roman land surface	(8) Probable basement destruction	(9) Archaeological Potential Roman c.A.D.43–c.450	(10) Archaeological Potential Anglo-Saxon c.450–1066	(11) Archaeological Potential Medieval 1066–c.1500
					In metres above O.D.					

310–315/805–810

Development Imminent

1	310–315 810–815	The Feathers public house 36 Tudor Street	3.2.72	Offices and shops	6·1	>1·5	L	Unknown, but occupation likely	Unknown	Part of the site of White Friars
2	315–320 805–810	City of London School for Girls, Guildhall School of Music and Drama 5/11 Tudor Street, John Carpenter Street	11.12.69	Offices	5·5	<1·5	(L) & (T)	Unknown, but occupation likely. River frontage	Unknown. River frontage	Part of the site of the Bishop of Salisbury's Inn. River frontage

310–315/810–815

Development Imminent

3	—	54/55 Fetter Lane	18.11.71	Offices	18·3	?	(P)	Suburban occupation. Possible cemetery	(Suburban occupation ?)	(Suburban occupation ?)
4	—	Daily Telegraph, 135 Fleet Street	23.9.65	Offices and industry [new scheme under discussion]	13·7	?	L, (P), (T)	(Suburban occupation and cemetery. Fort ?)	(Suburban occupation ?)	(Suburban occupation)
5	—	5/11 Fetter Lane, 8/11 Crane Court	29.4.71	Showroom and computer	15·2	?	(L)	(Suburban occupation and cemetery)	(Suburban occupation ?)	(Suburban occupation)
6	—	Land adjoining the Three Tuns public house, West Harding Street, Great New Street	22.7.71	Offices	16·8	?	—	Suburban occupation and cemetery	Suburban occupation ?	Suburban occupation
7	—	5/6 Crane Court	23.3.72	Reinstatement after fire damage	15·2	?	L	(Suburban occupation and cemetery)	(Suburban occupation ?)	(Suburban occupation)

No.	Grid ref	Address	Date	Proposed use	Area	?	Code			
8	—	9 Red Lion Court	3.2.72 O	Offices	15·2	?	(L)	Suburban occupation and cemetery	Suburban occupation ?	Suburban occupation
9	—	20/21 Red Lion Court	13.1.72 O	Offices	15·2	?	—	Suburban occupation and cemetery	Suburban occupation ?	Suburban occupation
10	—	4/12 Bell Yard	16.12.49	Offices [scheme probably abandoned]	15·2	?	—	Unknown	Unknown, probably unlikely	Suburban occupation
11	—	2/6 Salisbury Square, 23/24 Whitefriars Street, Hanging Sword Alley	11.6.64 C	No details	10·7	?	(L)	Suburban occupation and cemetery. Fort ?	(Suburban occupation ?)	(On the border between White Friars and the Bishop of Salisbury's Inn)
(1)	310–315 805–810	The Feathers public house, 36 Tudor Street	3.2.72	Offices and shops	6·1	>1·5	L	Unknown, but occupation likely	Unknown	Part of the site of White Friars Priory

Development probable in next five years

No.	Grid ref	Address	Date	Proposed use	Area	?	Code			
12	—	94/97 Fetter Lane	—	—	18·6	?	L	Suburban occupation. Possible cemetery	(Suburban occupation ?)	(Suburban occupation ?)

310–315/815–820

Development imminent

No.	Grid ref	Address	Date	Proposed use	Area	?	Code			
13	—	8 Holborn Circus, 102/112 Hatton Garden, 113/129 Holborn, 2 Leather Lane	O D P 17.2.72	Scheme under consideration	18·3	?	L & P	Suburban occupation and/or cemetery. Possible E.–W. road from Newgate	(Unknown)	(North of E.–W. road. Suburban occupation ?)
14	—	5/12 Holborn, 1/3 Furnival Street	O D P 15.3.71	Scheme under consideration	19·4	?	—	Suburban occupation and/or cemetery. Possible E.–W. road from Newgate	Unknown	South of E.–W. road. Suburban occupation ?

315–320/805–810

Development imminent

No.	Grid ref	Address	Date	Proposed use	Area	?	Code			
(2)	310–315 805–810	City of London School for Girls, Guildhall School of Music and Drama, 5/11 Tudor Street, John Carpenter Street	11.12.69	Offices	5·5	<1·5	(L) & (T)	Unknown, but occupation likely. River frontage	Unknown. River frontage	Part of the site of the Bishop of Salisbury's Inn. River frontage

(1) Ref. no.	(2) Other 500 m squares	(3) Address of site	(4) Date of planning permission	(5) Proposed development	(6) Approx. present land surface In metres above O.D.	(7) Approx. Roman land surface	(8) Probable basement destruction	(9) Archaeological Potential Roman c.A.D.43–c.450	(10) Archaeological Potential Anglo-Saxon c.450–1066	(11) Archaeological Potential Medieval 1066–c.1500
15	—	Mermaid Theatre site, Puddle Dock	14.1.71	—	4·6	S L	—	River frontage/foreshore	River frontage	River frontage
16	—	179 Queen Victoria Street	1950	Probably abandoned	7·6	S L	(T)	[Mouth of Fleet River]	[Mouth of Fleet River]	[Mouth of Fleet River]

Development probable in next five years

(1)	(2)	(3)	(4)	(5)	(6)	(7)	(8)	(9)	(10)	(11)
17	315–320 810–815	Site E. of New Bridge Street and S. of Ludgate Circus	—	Area outstanding from L.C.C. Development Plan 1962	6·7– 7·6	S L – 4·6	(L)	Mouth of Fleet river	Mouth of Fleet river	Between Blackfriars precinct and Fleet river
18	320–325 805–810	Telecommunications Centre, Queen Victoria Street	9.3.72	Excavations took place during 1972. Site crossed by road scheme	6·1	S L	—	River foreshore. Ship remains ?	River frontage	Site of second Baynard Castle
19	—	119/165 Queen Victoria Street, 227/242 Upper Thames Street	—	Part of North Bank scheme	6·1– 7·6	1·5– 6·1	(L)	N. of river frontage. Occupation ?	N. of river frontage. Occupation	Occupation
20	—	Sites E. and W. of Blackfriars Station, bounded by Queen Victoria Street	—	—	4·2– 6·7	SL – 1·5	(L), (P) & (T)	Mouth of Fleet river. Possible S. end of city wall	Mouth of Fleet river. Thames river frontage. Possible S. ends of both Roman and extended medieval city walls	Mouth of Fleet river. Thames river frontage, and part of Blackfriars precinct

315–320/810–815

Development imminent

(1)	(2)	(3)	(4)	(5)	(6)	(7)	(8)	(9)	(10)	(11)
21	—	14/23 Holborn Viaduct, 37/40 Farringdon Street	ODP 21.1.72	Scheme under consideration	7·9	SL – 4·6	(T)	[Beside Fleet river. Cemetery]	[Suburban occupation ?]	[Suburban occupation]
22	—	Fleetway House, 22/25 Farringdon Street, 1/2 Bear Alley	ODP 21.6.71	New application under consideration	6·4	SL – 4·6	L, P & T	[Beside Fleet river. Cemetery]	[Unknown]	[Unknown]

No.		Site	Date	Present use			Code			
23	—	Daily Express, 112/119 Fleet Street, Stage VIII; site bounded by Shoe Lane, Fleet Street, Poppins Court and St Bride Street	11.5.72	Offices, industry and shops	12·2	> 1·5	L, (P), (T)	[Suburban occupation, possible fort, cemetery]	[Suburban occupation ?]	[Suburban occupation]
24	—	Hutchinson House, 3/5 Friar Street, 2 Ireland Yard, Burgon Street	ODP 17.8.70	Scheme under consideration	12·2	9·1–10·7	(L)	Scattered occupation. Early burials ?	(Unknown)	(Within Blackfriars precinct. First site of Baynard Castle.)
25	—	13/16 New Bridge Street, 2 and 4 Tudor Street, 9 and 12 Bridewell Place	14.12.72	—	6·7	SL–1·5	(L) & (P)	On W. bank of Fleet river. Possible suburban occupation. Cemetery? Fort?	(Unknown)	(Bridewell Palace (1522))

Development probable in next five years

No.		Site	Date	Present use			Code			
(17) 315–320 805–810 — 26	—	Site E. of New Bridge Street and N. of Ludgate Circus	—	Area outstanding from L.C.C. Development Plan 1962	6·7–7·6	SL–4·6	(L) & (T)	Beside Fleet river. Cemetery. Fort ?	Beside Fleet river. Suburban occupation ?	Beside and across Fleet river. Just outside wall of Blackfriars precinct. Suburban occupation
27	—	S.W. of Ludgate Circus	—	Area outstanding from L.C.C. Development Plan 1962, roads scheme	7·6–9·1	SL–2·0	—	Suburban occupation. Fort ? Cemetery ? Road from Ludgate ?	Suburban occupation ?	Near Fleet river and E.–W. road. Suburban occupation
28	—	Site bounded by Ludgate Hill, St Paul's Church Yard, Godliman Street, Carter Lane, Waithman Street	—	Area outstanding from L.C.C. Development Plan 1962	9·1–15·2	4·6–>10·7	(L), (P), (T)	City wall, occupation and buildings. Road ? Early cemetery ?	City wall. Streets and occupation	Part of Blackfriars precinct, later course of city wall to W. of earlier line. First site of Baynard Castle ?

315–320/815–820

Development imminent

No.		Site	Date	Present use			Code			
29	—	18/19 Long Lane, 1/2 Hayne Street	5.2.70	Offices, storage, showroom	16·8	?	—	Unknown	Unknown	Saxon objects from S.W. of this area. Saxon potential unknown

(1) Ref. no.	(2) Other 500 m squares	(3) Address of site	(4) Date of planning permission	(5) Proposed development	(6) Approx. present land surface In metres above O.D.	(7) Approx. Roman land surface	(8) Probable basement destruction	(9) Archaeological Potential Roman c.A.D.43–c.450	(10) Archaeological Potential Anglo-Saxon c.450–1066	(11) Archaeological Potential Medieval 1066–c.1500
30	320–325 815–820	73/88 Long Lane, 8/12 Half Moon Court, 1/3 Cloth Street, 1/25A Middle Street, etc.	ODP 9.7.64	Offices, shops and commerce	16·8	?	(L)	Unknown, possible suburban occupation and/or cemetery	Saxon objects from S.W. of this area. Saxon potential unknown	Part of St Bartholomew Priory precinct
31	—	7/12 Hosier Lane	10.10.63	Probably abandoned. Offices and cold storage	17·4	?	(L) & (T)	Cemetery	Unknown	Suburban occupation. Site bounded by medieval E.–W. streets
32	—	24/30 West Smithfield, 14/21 Hosier Lane, 21/30 Cock Lane	ODP 20.9.71	Scheme under consideration	17·4	?	(L)	Cemetery	Unknown	Suburban occupation. Site bounded by medieval E.–W. streets
Development probable in next five years										
33	—	Site bounded by Long Lane, Cloth Fair, Rising Sun Court and Kinghorn Street	—	Outstanding from L.C.C. Development Plan 1962	16·5	?	—	Unknown, possible suburban occupation and/or cemetery	Saxon objects from S.W. of this area. Saxon potential unknown	Part of St Bartholomew Priory precinct
34	320–325 815–820	Site bounded by Kinghorn Street, Bartholomew Close and Cloth Fair	—	Outstanding from L.C.C. Development Plan 1962	16·5	?	—	Unknown, possible suburban occupation and/or cemetery	Saxon objects from S.W. of this area. Saxon potential unknown	Part of St Bartholomew Priory precinct
35	320–325 815–820	Large site E. of Little Britain and N. of Postman's Park	—	Outstanding from L.C.C. Development Plan 1962	15·2– 16·7	?	(L) & (T)	Cemetery ? and suburban occupation ? Early road W. from Cripplegate fort.	Suburban occupation	Part of St Bartholomew Priory precinct. Suburban occupation along Aldersgate Street

Development imminent

36	320–325 810–815	Site bounded by Cannon Street, Queen Victoria Street and Bread Street	ODP 16.7.71	Under consideration	14·6	9–10	(L)	Roman bath found on part of site 1906. Occupation and buildings likely	To. E. of Cannon Street hut-pits. Occupation. St Mildred, possible late Saxon church	Occupation. Church of St Mildred
37	—	63 Queen Victoria Street	24.9.64	Offices and commerce	14·3	9·1	(L)	Masonry and walls found to N.W. of site. Occupation and buildings likely	To E. of Cannon Street hut-pits. Occupation	Occupation
(18)	315–320 805–810	Telecommunications Centre, Queen Victoria Street	9.3.72	Excavations took place during 1972. Site crossed by road scheme	6·1	SL	—	River foreshore. Ship remains?	River frontage	Site of second Baynard Castle
38	—	17/21 Queenhithe	ODP 21.4.71	Refused 23.9.71	6·0	SL	(L)	River frontage. Wharves? Ship remains?	River frontage. Wharves. Probable use throughout Saxon period. Queenhithe?	River frontage. Wharves, warehouses. Queenhithe
	—	Bull Wharf Lane, rear of 16 Queenhithe	ODP 21.4.71							
39	—	62/64 Queen Street	9.7.70	Offices	7·6	2–5	L & (P)	Floor and wall foundations found to E. of site. Occupation and buildings likely	(To N. of site of St Martin in the Vintry, possible early Saxon church. Occupation)	(Occupation)
40	—	Site W. of St Nicholas Cole Abbey, Queen Victoria Street	—	Application made	12·2	7·6– 9·1	—	Wall found near site. Occupation and buildings likely	Near Cannon Street occupation area. Occupation	Beside medieval church of St Nicholas Cole Abbey and fronting medieval road to N. Occupation

Development probable in next five years

41	320–325 810–815	Site bounded by Queen Victoria Street, Cannon Street and Queen Street	—	Included in Corporation's road plans	12·2	7·6– 9·5	(L)	Walls and mosaic found to S. of site. Occupation and buildings likely. Early burials	Occupation	Occupation
42	—	Site bounded by Caldwell Yard, Upper Thames Street and Stew Lane	—	Outstanding from L.C.C. Development Plan 1962	6·1	SL	(L), (P)	River frontage. Wharves, ship remains?	River foreshore, wharves. Probable use throughout Saxon period	River frontage, wharves, warehouses

(1) Ref. no.	(2) Other 500 m squares	(3) Address of site	(4) Date of planning permission	(5) Proposed development	(6) Approx. present land surface	(7) Approx. Roman land surface	(8) Probable basement destruction	(9) Archaeological Potential Roman c.A.D.43–c.450	(10) Archaeological Potential Anglo-Saxon c.450–1066	(11) Archaeological Potential Medieval 1066–c.1500
					In metres above O.D.					
43	—	Site bounded by Upper Thames Street, Stew Lane, Smith's Wharf and Bull Wharf Lane	—	Outstanding from L.C.C. Development Plan 1962	6·1	SL	(L)	River frontage. Wharves.	River foreshore, wharves. Probable use throughout Saxon period. Queenhithe ?	River frontage, wharves, warehouses. Queenhithe to S.
44	—	181/190 Upper Thames Street, 40/41 Queen Street, 1 Skinners Lane	—	Outstanding from L.C.C. Development Plan 1962	7·3—9·1	1·5—4·0	(L)	Walls and pavement found in vicinity. Occupation and buildings likely	Occupation	Occupation. Church of St James Garlickhithe
45	—	Site bounded by Queenhithe, Kennet Wharf and Bull Wharf	—	Outstanding from L.C.C. Development Plan 1962	4·6	SL	L	Thames foreshore. Ship remains ?	River frontage. Wharves. Probable use throughout Saxon period	(River frontage, wharves, warehouses)
46	—	Site N. and E. of Kennet Wharf	—	Outstanding from L.C.C. Development Plan 1962	4·6	SL	(T)	Thames foreshore. Ship remains ?	River frontage. Wharves. Probable use throughout Saxon period	River frontage, wharves, warehouses
47	—	65/66 Queen Street, 1/4 College Hill	—	Application received	9·1	6·1	L	Walls and mosaic found in vicinity. Buildings and occupation likely	(Occupation probable)	(Occupation)

320–325/810–815

Development imminent

(1) Ref. no.	(2) Other 500 m squares	(3) Address of site	(4) Date of planning permission	(5) Proposed development	(6) Approx. present land surface	(7) Approx. Roman land surface	(8) Probable basement destruction	(9) Archaeological Potential Roman c.A.D.43–c.450	(10) Archaeological Potential Anglo-Saxon c.450–1066	(11) Archaeological Potential Medieval 1066–c.1500
48	—	90/91 and 100 Wood Street	3.6.71	Offices	15·5	>12·2	(P)	Cripplegate fort interior. Beside street. Near S. gate	Just W. of St Alban's church and W. of the traditional site of Ethelbert's Palace. Occupation ?	(Occupation)
49	—	GPO, St Martin's le Grand	Circular 100	Site vacant	17·7	>12·2	L	Early cemetery and later occupation ?	(Late Saxon finds to E. of site. Occupation ?)	(Part of grounds of College of St Martin le Grand. Site of Shambles to S. Occupation)

50	—	Guildhall redevelopment scheme	—	15·2	9–10	—	Building now demolished	Unknown, but occupation probable	Roman foundations in vinicity. Occupation and buildings likely	Occupation
51	—	12/16 Mumford Court, 7/8 Milk Street	11.6.70	15·2	9–10	—	Corporation development delayed for archaeological excavations	Occupation	E.–W. street	Occupation
52	—	19/28 Watling Street, 5/9 Watling Court, 39/53 Cannon Street, 11/14 Salter Court	ODP 24.8.71	15·2	9–10	(L)	Scheme under consideration	W. of St Mary Aldermary, of possible late Saxon date. Occupation	Road, with structural remains to E. and W. of site. Occupation and buildings likely	Occupation
53	—	30/32 Watling Street	22.7.71	15·2	9–10	(L)	Offices	At N.W. corner of St Mary Aldermary church. Occupation	Road and structural remains near site. Occupation and buildings likely	Occupation
(36)	320–325 805–810	Site bounded by Cannon Street, Queen Victoria Street and Bread Street	ODP 16.7.71	14·6	9–10	(L)	Under consideration	To E. of Cannon Street hut-pits. Occupation. St Mildred, possible late Saxon church	Roman bath found on part of site 1906. Occupation and buildings likely	Occupation. Church of St Mildred

Development probable in next five years

54	—	10 King Edward Street, 71/76 Little Britain	—	16·7	>12·2	(L)	Road proposal running parallel to St Martin le Grand	W. of area of finds at St Martin le Grand. Occupation ? City wall. Ditch ?	Crosses line of city wall. Extra-mural cemetery ? Occupation probable within and without walls	Part of precinct of College of St Martin le Grand. City wall. Ditch
55	—	Site N. of St Vedast's Church and E. of Foster Lane	—	16·7	>12·2	(L)	Outstanding from L.C.C. Development Plan 1962	Late Saxon finds to W. of area. Occupation probable	Occupation	To N. of St Vedast's church, bounded to W. by early street. Occupation
56	325–330 810–815	Guildhall Art Gallery, Portland House	—	15·2	7·6– 10·0	(L)	Phase V of Guildhall Development Scheme	Unknown. Occupation ?	Probably crossed by Walbrook tributaries. Occupation ?	Occupation
57	325–330 810–815	Courts Block Site bounded by Guildhall Yard and Gresham Street	—	14·6	7·6– 9·1	(L)	Phase II Phase III Guildhall Development Scheme	Unknown. Occupation ?	Probably crossed by Walbrook tributaries. Occupation ?	Occupation

(1) Ref. no.	(2) Other 500 m squares	(3) Address of site	(4) Date of planning permission	(5) Proposed development	(6) Approx. present land surface In metres above O.D.	(7) Approx. Roman land surface	(8) Probable basement destruction	(9) Archaeological Potential Roman c.A.D.43–c.450	(10) Archaeological Potential Anglo-Saxon c.450–1066	(11) Archaeological Potential Medieval 1066–c.1500
58	—	Site N. of Cheapside, between Wood Street and Gutter Lane, W. to Cheapside House	—	Outstanding from L.C.C. Development Plan 1962	17·5	10·7–12·2	(L) (T)	Walls and floor found to N. of site. Occupation, and streets likely to S. and W.	Early Saxon find in vicinity. On West Cheap. Early and late Saxon occupation likely	Site of church of St Peter, Wood Street. Occupation
59	—	1/6 Milk Street	—	Outstanding from L.C.C. Development Plan 1962	16·8	10–11	(L)	Possibility of E.–W. road. Site to N. of Cheapside baths. Occupation and buildings likely	Saxon finds to N. of site. Occupation	Occupation
60	—	1/9 Bow Lane, Bow Churchyard, 72/77 Watling Street	ODP 26.11.70	Outstanding from D.P. 1962. Scheme refused permission 11.3.71	16·8	9·1–10·7	(L)	Tessellated pavement found to W. of site. Occupation and buildings likely, with road to S.	Occupation. S. of possible late Saxon church of St Mary le Bow	Occupation
(41)	320–325 805–810	Site bounded by Queen Victoria Street, Cannon Street and Queen Street	—	Included in road proposals	12·2	7·6–9·5	(L)	Walls and mosaic found to S. of site. Occupation and buildings likely. Early burials	Occupation	Occupation

320–325/815–820

Development imminent

(1) Ref. no.	(2) Other 500 m squares	(3) Address of site	(4) Date of planning permission	(5) Proposed development	(6) Approx. present land surface In metres above O.D.	(7) Approx. Roman land surface	(8) Probable basement destruction	(9) Archaeological Potential Roman c.A.D.43–c.450	(10) Archaeological Potential Anglo-Saxon c.450–1066	(11) Archaeological Potential Medieval 1066–c.1500
(30)	315–320 815–820	73/88 Long Lane, 8/12 Half Moon Court, 1/3 Cloth Street, 1/25A Middle Street, 1/15, 19/31 Newbury Street, 12/13 Kinghorn Street, 34/39 Bartholomew Close, 1/7 Bartholomew Place	ODP 9.7.64	Offices, commerce and shops	16·8	?	(L)	Unknown. Possible suburban occupation and/or cemetery	Saxon objects found S.W. of this area. Saxon potential unknown	Part of St Bartholomew Priory precinct
61	—	Gloucester House extension, Little Britain	1964	Extension to building	16·8	?	—	Cemetery ?	Unknown	On S. edge of St Bartholomew Priory precinct

Development probable in next five years

	Grid ref	Site		Development						Notes
(34)	315–320 815–820	Site bounded by Kinghorn Street, Bartholomew Close and Cloth Fair	—	Outstanding from L.C.C. Development Plan 1962	16·5	?	—	Unknown. Possible suburban occupation and/or cemetery	Saxon objects from S.W. of this area. Saxon potential unknown	Part of St Bartholomew Priory precinct
(35)	315–320 815–820	Large site E. of Little Britain and N. of Postman's Park	—	Outstanding from L.C.C. Development Plan 1962	15·2–16·7	?	(L) & (T)	Cemetery? and suburban occupation? Early road W. from Cripplegate fort	Suburban occupation	Part of St Bartholomew Priory precinct. Suburban occupation along Aldersgate Street

325–330/805–810

Development imminent

	Site		Development	Depth		Code	Roman	Saxon	
62	—	27/28 Clement's Lane	22.1.71	Offices	15·2	9–10	T	[Walling and pavement in vicinity and probable evidence of glass-making. N.–S. road, occupation and buildings likely]	[Scatter of late Saxon finds on sites nearby. Occupation]	[Occupation]
63	—	39/40 Lombard Street, 26, 29, 30 and 32 Gracechurch Street, 2/3 Lombard Court	23.9.71	Offices and bank	16·4	11–12	L & (T)	Pavements and walling in vicinity. Occupation and buildings likely	(Some late Saxon finds in vinicity. Occupation)	(Occupation)
64	—	Bush Lane House, 1/8 Bush Lane, The Dyers Arms, 78, 80/84 Cannon Street	17.2.72	Offices. Excavations took place in basement of building before demolition, 1972	7·4	4–7	L	Roman palace	Occupation	(Occupation)
65	—	110/114 Cannon Street, 1/4 Martin Lane, 24/27 Laurence Pountney Lane	ODP 1970	—	14·6	6–9	L & (P)	Walling and pavement in vicinity. Occupation, buildings and early cemetery likely	(Occupation probable)	(Occupation)
66	—	Island site bounded by Arthur Street, Upper Thames Street and King William Street	ODP 8.4.71	Scheme under consideration	6·1	1·5–5·0	(L), (P), (T)	(Traces of timber construction found on site. N.–S. road. Possible wharf. Occupation likely)	(Occupation)	

(1) Ref. no.	(2) Other 500 m squares	(3) Address of site	(4) Date of planning permission	(5) Proposed development	(6) Approx. present land surface In metres above O.D.	(7) Approx. Roman land surface	(8) Probable basement destruction	(9) Archaeological Potential Roman c.A.D.43–c.450	(10) Archaeological Potential Anglo-Saxon c.450–1066	(11) Archaeological Potential Medieval 1066–c.1500
67	—	104/106, 107/108 Upper Thames Street, Seal House, Exploration House, Swan Lane, 10 Fishmongers Hall Street	ODP 4.10.70	Scheme under consideration	6·1	SL–1·0	(L)	River frontage, wharves, ship remains ?	River frontage, wharves. Silver hoard in vicinity. Occupation likely throughout Saxon period	River frontage, wharves. Occupation
68	330–335 805–810	111/129 Lower Thames Street and Billingsgate Buildings	—	Road widening	6·1	1·5	(L) & (T)	Walls and pavement found in vicinity. Occupation and buildings likely. Possible bridge approach roads	N. of St Magnus and St Botolph churches. Occupation. Possible bridge approaches	Near bridge approaches. Occupation
69	330–335 805–810	Billingsgate Market, New Fresh Wharf, Lower Thames Street	1972	Approved since 30.9.72	6·1	SL	(L) & (T)	River frontage, wharves, ship remains ? Possible bridge abutments	River frontage. Site of St Botolph, possible late Saxon church. Near St Magnus church. Occupation likely throughout Saxon period	River frontage, wharves, medieval bridge abutment. Site of St Botolph church. Occupation

Development probable in next five years

(1) Ref. no.	(2) Other 500 m squares	(3) Address of site	(4) Date of planning permission	(5) Proposed development	(6) Approx. present land surface	(7) Approx. Roman land surface	(8) Probable basement destruction	(9) Archaeological Potential Roman	(10) Archaeological Potential Anglo-Saxon	(11) Archaeological Potential Medieval
70	—	Walbrook River Club, Cousin Lane	—	Application under consideration	6·1	SL	—	River frontage. Mouth of the Walbrook. Ship remains ?	River frontage. Mouth of the Walbrook	River frontage. Dowgate
71	330–335 805–810	9/21 Eastcheap, 1/10 Philpot Lane, 5/12 Fenchurch Street	—	Application 27.7.72, not yet approved	15·2–16·8	10–11	(L) & (T)	Evidence of buildings in vicinity. Occupation and buildings likely. Roads to E. and S.	Occupation. East Cheap	Occupation

325–330/810–815

Development imminent

(1) Ref. no.	(2) Other 500 m squares	(3) Address of site	(4) Date of planning permission	(5) Proposed development	(6) Approx. present land surface	(7) Approx. Roman land surface	(8) Probable basement destruction	(9) Archaeological Potential Roman	(10) Archaeological Potential Anglo-Saxon	(11) Archaeological Potential Medieval
72	—	41/43 Moorgate, 67/71 Coleman Street	23.3.72 C	Offices	13·1	9–10	—	Brick pavement and votive plaque found to N. of site, stream nearby. Occupation ?	Unknown. Occupation ?	Little known in area. Medieval road to W. of site. Potential unknown.

No.	Grid	Address	Ref.	Development						
73	—	12/18 Austin Friars, 21/22 Great Winchester Street	ODP 30.11.71	Scheme under consideration	13·4	7–9	(L) & (T)	Crossed by stream, evidence of occupation to S. of site	St Olave Broad Street, in vicinity, of possible late Saxon date, site unknown	(Part of Austin Friars precinct)
74	—	30/33 Coleman Street	ODP 2.7.71	Scheme under consideration	13·7	7–9	(?)	Possibly near stream. Little known of this area.	Late Saxon finds to N. Occupation?	N. of site of St Stephen de Coleman Street. Occupation
75	—	2/8 Angel Court, 1/2 Copthall Buildings, 1/5, 11/13 Copthall Court, 30/32 Throgmorton Street	ODP 9.2.72	Scheme under consideration	13·1	4·5–8·0	(L)	Two tributaries of Walbrook probably cross site. Little known of this area. Occupation?	Unknown, but possible occupation along Throgmorton Street	(Little known. Occupation to S.)
76	—	67 Lombard Street, 18/25 Birchin Lane, 1 Castle Court, Bengal Court	3.2.72 C	Offices	16·5	>10·7	(L) & (T)	(Road metalling observed 1935. Pavement and walls near site. W. margin of forum area. Occupation and buildings likely)	(Near All Hallows, Lombard Street, certain late Saxon church, and St Edmund, possible late Saxon church. Occupation)	(Occupation)

Development probable in next five years

No.	Grid	Address	Ref.	Development						
77	—	3/7 Throgmorton Avenue, 23/25 Great Winchester Street	—	Application not yet approved	13·4	7·6–9·1	(T)	(Possible small road found near site, 1880. Probably crossed by Walbrook tributaries)	(Unknown, but St Olave, Broad Street, in vicinity, possible late Saxon church)	(Just outside precinct of Austin Friars)
(56)	320–325 810–815	Guildhall Art Gallery and Portland House	—	Phase V of Guildhall Development Scheme	15·2	7·6–10·0	(L)	Probably crossed by Walbrook tributaries. Occupation?	Unknown. Occupation?	Occupation
(57)	320–325 810–815	Site bounded by Guildhall Yard and Gresham Street;	—	Phase III of Guildhall Development Scheme	14·6	7·6–9·1	(L)	Probably crossed by Walbrook tributaries. Occupation?	Unknown. Occupation?	Occupation
		Courts Block	—	Phase II						
78	—	2/6 Austin Friars	—	Application not yet approved	13·7	7·6–9·1	P	Evidence of occupation to N. and S. of site. Occupation likely. Early cemetery?	(Unknown)	(On edge of Austin Friars precinct)
79	330–335 810–815	41/53 Threadneedle Street, 2/17 Old Broad Street	ODP 16.4.70	Scheme under consideration	13·7–15·2	9·1–10·7	L & (T)	Tessellated pavement found at no.53. N.–S. road. Early cemetery?	(Occupation. Early street frontages)	(Occupation. Hospital of St Anthony)

(1) Ref. no.	(2) Other 500 m squares	(3) Address of site	(4) Date of planning permission	(5) Proposed development	(6) Approx. present land surface In metres above O.D.	(7) Approx. Roman land surface	(8) Probable basement destruction	(9) Archaeological Potential Roman c.A.D.43–c.450	(10) Archaeological Potential Anglo-Saxon c.450–1066	(11) Archaeological Potential Medieval 1066–c.1500
80	—	Site bounded by Bucklersbury, Queen Victoria Street and Sise Lane	—	Outstanding from L.C.C. Development Plan 1962	13·7	7·6–10·0	(L) & (T)	Crossed by E.–W. road and course of Walbrook tributary. Occupation and buildings likely	Site of possible late Saxon church of St Sythe, later St Benet. Occupation	Site of church of St Benet Shorehog. Occupation

325–330/815–820

Development imminent

(1) Ref. no.	(2) Other 500 m squares	(3) Address of site	(4) Date of planning permission	(5) Proposed development	(6) Approx. present land surface	(7) Approx. Roman land surface	(8) Probable basement destruction	(9) Archaeological Potential Roman	(10) Archaeological Potential Anglo-Saxon	(11) Archaeological Potential Medieval
81	—	89/135 Moorgate, 10/28 Moorfields	ODP 1970	—	13·7	>7·6	L	Cemetery Possible tributary of Walbrook	Unknown, but finds to S.E.	Negative ?
82	—	18/25 Eldon Street	24.9.59	Offices and shops	12·8	>6·1	L	Cemetery. Walbrook tributary	Negative ?	(Negative ?)

330–335/805–810

Development imminent

(1) Ref. no.	(2) Other 500 m squares	(3) Address of site	(4) Date of planning permission	(5) Proposed development	(6) Approx. present land surface	(7) Approx. Roman land surface	(8) Probable basement destruction	(9) Archaeological Potential Roman	(10) Archaeological Potential Anglo-Saxon	(11) Archaeological Potential Medieval
83	330–335 810–815	77/82 Gracechurch Street, 1/4 & 10/12 Bulls Head Passage, 'The Swan', Ship Tavern Passage	ODP 18.6.71	Scheme under consideration	16·8	>10·7	(L) & (T)	Site within Roman Forum. Floors of various dates observed to N. of site. Occupation and buildings	(Occupation)	(Occupation)
84	—	27/30 Lime Street	—	Application made 2.8.72, not yet approved	16·8	>10·7	—	On edge of Forum area, early buildings and occupation likely	Pottery finds in vicinity. Occupation	Occupation
85	—	141/142 Fenchurch Street	21.9.72	—	16·7	>10·7	P	Early buildings and occupation likely	(Pottery finds in vicinity. Occupation)	(Occupation)

No.	Grid ref.	Date	Development			Code	Roman period	Late Saxon period	Category
86	330–335 810–815	22.10.64	Offices and public houses	15·9	>10·7	L	Early buildings and occupation likely. Possible granary or warehouse found to S. of site	Late Saxon finds in vicinity. Occupation. On early street frontage	(Occupation)
87	—	23.9.71	Offices	13·7	9·1– 10·7	L, P & T	(Pavement and part of a sculpture found in Seething Lane, otherwise little recorded in area. Occupation likely)	[Near St Olave, possible late Saxon church. Occupation ?]	[Occupation]
88	335–340 805–810	22.7.71	Offices	12·5	9– 10·7	L	Little recorded in area. Occupation ? Early cemetery ?	(Unknown)	(Occupation)
89	335–340 805–810	3.2.72 C	Offices	12·5	9–10	(L)	Little recorded in area. Occupation ? Early cemetery ?	Unknown	Occupation
90	—	ODP 18.8.70	Scheme under consideration	15·2	9–11	(L) & (P)	Little recorded in area. Possible structural remains to S. of site. Occupation and buildings likely	On East Cheap. Occupation likely at least throughout late Saxon period	Occupation
91	335–340 805–810	13.1.72 C	Offices	13·7	9–10	(L) & (T)	Little recorded in area. Unknown	(Unknown)	(Part of precinct of Crutched Friars)
92	—	24.7.58	Offices	7·6	5–7	—	To W. of private baths and house. Occupation and buildings likely and sub-Roman occupation possible	Occupation throughout Saxon period probable	Occupation
93	—	ODP 9.3.72	Scheme under consideration. Roman house and baths, already excavated, to be preserved in new scheme	9·7	6·1	(L)	Further buildings likely	Occupation	Occupation
94	—	15.10.70	Offices	9·8	7·6– 9·1	(T)	Evidence of Roman building in vicinity, occupation likely	To W. of All Hallows Church. Occupation	Occupation

Site references:
86 — 120/124 Fenchurch Street
87 — 34/38 Crutched Friars, 2/3 New London Street, 9 Railway Place
88 — 3/5 Lloyds Avenue
89 — 51/53 Crutched Friars, 10 Lloyds Avenue
90 — 23/39 Eastcheap, 10/13 Rood Lane and 14 Philpot Lane
91 — 1/3 Pepys Street and Savage Gardens
92 — 14/16 St Mary at Hill
93 — 3, 6/8 St Dunstan's Lane, 27 St Mary at Hill and Coal Exchange adjacent
94 — Unit 7, Block F, Lower Thames Street, E. of Byward Street

(1) Ref. no.	(2) Other 500 m squares	(3) Address of site	(4) Date of planning permission	(5) Proposed development	(6) Approx. present land surface In metres above O.D.	(7) Approx. Roman land surface	(8) Probable basement destruction	(9) Archaeological Potential Roman c.A.D. 43–c.450	(10) Archaeological Potential Anglo-Saxon c.450–1066	(11) Archaeological Potential Medieval 1066–c.1500
(68)	325–330 805–810	111/129 Lower Thames Street and Billingsgate Buildings	—	Road widening	6·1	1·5	(L) & (T)	Walls and pavement found in vicinity. Occupation and buildings likely. Possible bridge approach roads	N. of St Magnus and St Botolph churches. Occupation. Possible bridge approaches	Near bridge approaches. Occupation
(69)	325–330 805–810	Billingsgate Market, New Fresh Wharf, Lower Thames Street	1972	Approved since 30.9.72	6·1	SL	(L) & (T)	River frontage, wharves, ship remains ? Possible bridge abutments	River frontage. Site of St Botolph, possible late Saxon church. Near St Magnus church. Occupation likely throughout Saxon period	River frontage, wharves. Medieval bridge abutment. Site of St Botolph church. Occupation
95	—	19/21 St Dunstan's Hill, 8/9, 12/13 Harp Lane, part of 78/83 Lower Thames Street	17.9.70	Offices and public house	6·1– 10·6	3·0– 6·1	(P)	House and baths found to W. of site. Occupation and buildings likely. Sub-Roman occupation possible	Occupation likely throughout Saxon period	Occupation
96	—	Custom House, Wool Quays, Lower Thames Street	ODP 6.1.72	Scheme under consideration	5·7	SL	(L) & (P)	River frontage, wharves, ship remains ?	River frontage, wharves	River frontage, wharves

Development probable in next five years

(1) Ref. no.	(2) Other 500 m squares	(3) Address of site	(4) Date of planning permission	(5) Proposed development	(6) Approx. present land surface	(7) Approx. Roman land surface	(8) Probable basement destruction	(9) Archaeological Potential Roman	(10) Archaeological Potential Anglo-Saxon	(11) Archaeological Potential Medieval
(71)	325–330 805–810	9/21 Eastcheap, 1/10 Philpot Lane, 5/12 Fenchurch Street	—	Application 27.7.72, not yet approved	15·2– 16·8	10–11	(L) & (T)	Evidence of buildings in vicinity. Occupation and buildings likely. Roads to E. and S.	Occupation. East Cheap	Occupation
97	330–335 810–815	2/5 Fen Court	—	Outstanding from L.C.C. Development Plan 1962	15·8	>10·7	L	Early buildings and occupation likely	Pottery finds in vicinity. Occupation	Occupation
98	330–335 810–815	115/117 Fenchurch Street, 14 Billiter Street	—	Outstanding from L.C.C. Development Plan 1962	15·2	>10·7	(L) & (T)	Wall found to E. of site. Little recorded in area. Occupation likely	Pottery finds in vicinity. Occupation. On early street frontage	(Site of Ironmongers Hall on part of site. Occupation)

No.	Grid	Site	Date	Development						
99	330–335 810–815	Lloyd's Registry and site to S.W.	14.1.71 C	Scheme abandoned for the present	15·2	9·1–10·7	(L)	Little recorded in area. Road to Aldgate ?	Pottery finds from area. Occupation. On early street frontage	Occupation. Site of church of St Katherine de Coleman already partially recorded
100	—	P.L.A., Trinity Square	3.10.72	Alterations probably do not involve site clearance	14	9·1–10·7	L	Little recorded in area. Possible E.–W. road. Occupation ?	(Occupation ?)	(Occupation ?)
101	—	Site bounded by St Dunstan's Hill, Harp Lane, Cross Lane, and Great Tower Street	—	Outstanding from L.C.C. Development Plan 1962	7·6 13·2	5– 9·1	(L)	Pavement found near site, otherwise little known. Possible E.–W. road. Early cemetery ?	Occupation	Occupation
102	—	15/18 St Dunstan's Hill	—	Outstanding from L.C.C. Development Plan 1962	7·6	5–6	(T)	Near St Dunstan's. Wall and tesserae found on part of site	Occupation	Near St Dunstan's church. Occupation

330–335/810–815

Development imminent

No.	Grid	Site	Date	Development						
103	330–335 815–820	50/67 Old Broad Street, 27/42 Wormwood Street, The Kings Arms public house, 1/8 Bishopgate Churchyard	29.4.71	Offices, shops, public house and restaurant	13·1	7·6– 9·1	(L) & (P)	(Site crosses city wall. Ditches ? Cemetery)	(Site crosses city wall. Ditches. Potential otherwise unknown)	(Site crosses city wall. In city ditch. On S. edge of precinct of hospital of St Mary of Bethlehem)
104	330–335 815–820	142/150 Bishopsgate, 1/11 Devonshire Row	ODP 3.3.71	Scheme under consideration	15·2	7·6– 9·1	(T)	Near Bishopsgate road. Suburban occupation ? Cemetery	Suburban occupation	Occupation
105	—	56A/60 Houndsditch	ODP 17.3.71	No planning permission yet	14·3	9–10	L	Line of wall at S.W. of site. Ditches	Line of wall crossing site. Ditches ?	(Line of wall crossing site. In city ditch)
106	—	T.A. Centre, 2 Borer's Passage	—	To be demolished. No application made yet	15·2	9–10	—	Outside city wall. Suburban occupation ? Cemetery	Unknown	Suburban occupation ?
107	—	105/108 Old Broad Street	ODP 1970	Scheme not yet approved	13·4	7·6– 9·0	L	Little known in area. Early cemetery ?	Late Saxon find in vicinity. On early street frontage. Occupation likely	(Part of Austin Friars precinct. Occupation on frontage ?)

(1) Ref. no.	(2) Other 500 m squares	(3) Address of site	(4) Date of planning permission	(5) Proposed development	(6) Approx. present land surface In metres above O.D.	(7) Approx. Roman land surface	(8) Probable basement destruction	(9) Archaeological Potential Roman c.A.D.43–c.450	(10) Archaeological Potential Anglo-Saxon c.450–1066	(11) Archaeological Potential Medieval 1066–c.1500
108	— —	34 Great St Helens, 35/38 Great St Helens, 42/50 Bishopsgate	25.7.68 ODP 17.2.72	Offices Scheme under consideration	16·5	9–10	(L)	Mosaic pavement to S. of site, otherwise little known in area. N.–S. road probable. Occupation and buildings likely	On early street frontage. Occupation likely	On edge of St Helen's Priory precinct. Occupation
109	—	36/40 St Mary Axe	—	Application received	13·7	10·7	T	[Tessellated pavement and walls found in vicinity. Occupation and buildings likely]	[Unknown]	[Occupation]
110	—	55/59 St Mary Axe	5.3.70	Offices	14·3	10	(L)	Tessellated pavement and walls found in vicinity. Occupation and buildings likely	Unknown	Occupation
111	—	10/11 Goring Street, 47/56 Houndsditch, 66/70 St Mary Axe	25.2.71 C	Offices	14·3	>10·7	(L)	Line of city wall to S.W. of site. Ditches	Line of city wall to S.W. of site. Ditch?	Line of city wall to S.W. of site. Ditch?
112	—	2/26 Bishopsgate, 145/146 (part) and 149/159 Leadenhall Street	ODP 3.2.71	Scheme under consideration	17·1	>10·7	(L) & (T)	Little recorded in area. Mosaic found to N. Likely to contain major structures, and early occupation	(Occupation? On early street frontage. Near St Peter Cornhill)	(Occupation)
113	335–340 810–815	Site bounded by Creechurch Lane and Place, St James Passage, Duke's Place, 26 Creechurch Lane	2.10.69	Offices	16·4	>10·7	(L) & (P)	Little recorded in area. Site crosses city wall and ditches. Occupation?	Crosses city wall and ditches. Otherwise unknown	Part of precinct of Priory of the Holy Trinity. Site extends across city wall and ditches
114	—	109/114 Fenchurch Street, 17/18 Billiter Street	13.1.72 C	Offices	15·2	>10·7	(L) & (T)	Little recorded in area. Occupation and buildings likely	Late Saxon finds to W. of site. Occupation likely on early street frontage	Occupation
	—	42/49 Leadenhall Street, 22/28 Billiter Street	23.9.71	Offices, shops, and public house						

No.		Site	Application	Proposed use			(L) & (T)			
(83)	330–335 805–810	77/82 Gracechurch Street, 1/4 and 10/12 Bulls Head Passage, 'The Swan', Ship Tavern Passage	ODP 18.6.71	Scheme under consideration	16·8	>10·7	(L) & (T)	Site within Roman Forum. Floors of various dates observed to N. of site. Occupation and buildings	(Occupation)	(Occupation)
115	—	8/13 Lime Street, 2/4 Beehive Passage	3.2.72 C	Offices	17·3	>10·7	(L)	To E. of Forum. Major structures and early occupation likely	Late Saxon finds in vicinity. Occupation	Occupation
(86)	330–335 805–810	120/124 Fenchurch Street	22.10.64	Offices and public house	15·9	>10·7	L	Early buildings and occupation likely. Possible granary or warehouse found to S. of site	Late Saxon finds in vicinity. Occupation. On early street frontage	(Occupation)
116	—	99/100 Fenchurch Street	1969	—	15·8	>10·7	—	Little recorded in area. Road to Aldgate ? Occupation likely	Pottery find in vicinity. Occupation likely. On early street frontage	Occupation
117	—	78/79 Fenchurch Street	13.1.72	Offices, shops, commerce and residential	15·8	>10·7	—	Tile floor and walls found to N.E. of site. Road to Aldgate ? Occupation and buildings likely	Pottery find in vicinity. Occupation likely. On early street frontage	Occupation

Development probable in next five years

No.		Site	Application	Proposed use			(L) & (T)			
118	—	Exchange Buildings, 115/117 Houndsditch	—	Application received	15·2	9–10	—	Outside city wall. Potential unknown	Outside city wall and ditch. Potential unknown	Outside city wall and ditch. Suburban occupation ?
119	—	46/54 St Mary Axe, 1/16A Bevis Marks, 11/12 and 15/18 Bury Street	—	Road scheme	14·3	10·7	(L)	Pavement found at N. end of St Mary Axe. Occupation and buildings likely	Unknown	Occupation ?
(79)	325–330 810–815	41/53 Threadneedle Street, 2/17 Old Broad Street	ODP 16.4.70	Scheme under consideration	13·7– 15·2	9·1– 10·7	L & (T)	Tessellated pavement found at no.53. N.–S. road. Early cemetery ?	(Occupation. Early street frontages)	(Occupation. Hospital of St Anthony)
120	—	70/80 Leadenhall Street, 32/40 Mitre Street	—	Outstanding from L.C.C. Development Plan 1962	16·8	>10·7	(L)	Traces of early timber buildings found to E. and ditch of early fort. Occupation and buildings likely	Occupation ? On early street frontages	Part of precinct of Priory of the Holy Trinity, including church

(1) Ref. no.	(2) Other 500 m squares	(3) Address of site	(4) Date of planning permission	(5) Proposed development	(6) Approx. present land surface (In metres above O.D.)	(7) Approx. Roman land surface	(8) Probable basement destruction	(9) Archaeological Potential Roman c.A.D.43–c.450	(10) Archaeological Potential Anglo-Saxon c.450–1066	(11) Archaeological Potential Medieval 1066–c.1500
(97)	330–335 805–810	2/5 Fen Court	—	Outstanding from L.C.C. Development Plan 1962	15·8	>10·7	L	Early buildings and occupation likely	Pottery finds in vicinity. Occupation	Occupation
(98)	330–335 805–810	115/117 Fenchurch Street, 14 Billiter Street	—	Outstanding from L.C.C. Development Plan 1962	15·2	>10·7	(L) & (T)	Wall found to E. of site. Little recorded in area. Occupation likely	Pottery finds in vicinity. Occupation. On early street frontage	(Site of Ironmongers Hall on part of site. Occupation)
(99)	330–335 805–810	Lloyd's Registry and site to S.W.	14.1.71 C	Scheme abandoned for the present	15·2	9·1– 10·7	(L)	Little recorded in area. Road to Aldgate ?	Pottery finds from area. Occupation. On early street frontage	Occupation. Site of church of St Katherine de Coleman already partially recorded

330–335/815–820

Development imminent

(1) Ref. no.	(2) Other 500 m squares	(3) Address of site	(4) Date of planning permission	(5) Proposed development	(6) Approx. present land surface (In metres above O.D.)	(7) Approx. Roman land surface	(8) Probable basement destruction	(9) Archaeological Potential Roman c.A.D.43–c.450	(10) Archaeological Potential Anglo-Saxon c.450–1066	(11) Archaeological Potential Medieval 1066–c.1500
121	—	215/227 Bishopsgate	28.5.64	Offices	14·0	?	—	Outside city wall. Probably beyond cemetery area. Negative ?	Negative ?	Suburban occupation ?
122	—	262/272 Bishopsgate, part of George and Catherine Wheel Alley, 260A, 262, 262A, 262C Bishopsgate	ODP 6.5.71	New application received	14·0	?	(L)	Outside city wall. Probably beyond cemetery area. Negative ?	Negative ?	Part of precinct of new hospital of St Mary Spital. Suburban occupation
(103)	330–335 810–815	50/67 Old Broad Street, 27/42 Wormwood Street, The Kings Arms public house, 1/8 Bishopsgate Churchyard	29.4.71	Offices, shops, public house and restaurant	13·1	7·6– 9·1	(L) & (P)	(Site crosses city wall. Ditches ? Cemetery)	(Site crosses city wall. Ditches. Potential otherwise unknown)	(Site crosses city wall. In city ditch. On S. edge of precinct of hospital of St Mary of Bethlehem)
123	—	69 Old Broad Street	27.4.62	Offices and residential	13·1	7·6– 9·1	L	Cemetery	Unknown, but suburban occupation probable	(S. part of precinct of hospital of St Mary of Bethlehem. City ditch ?)

(104)	330–335 / 810–815	142/150 Bishopsgate, 1/11 Devonshire Row	ODP 3.3.71	Scheme under consideration	15·2	7·6–9·1	(T)	Near Bishopsgate road. Suburban occupation? Cemetery	Suburban occupation	Occupation

335–340/805–810

Development imminent

(88)	330–335 / 805–810	3/5 Lloyds Avenue	22.7.71	Offices	12·5	9–10·7	L	Little recorded in area. Occupation? Early cemetery?	(Unknown)	(Occupation)
(89)	330–335 / 805–810	51/53 Crutched Friars, 10 Lloyds Avenue	3.2.72 C	Offices	12·5	9–10	(L)	Little recorded in area. Occupation? Early cemetery?	Unknown	Occupation
124	—	52/56 Minories	25.2.71	Offices and showrooms	14·6	9–10	—	Near Goodmans Fields burial area. Cemetery	Unknown. Negative?	Suburban occupation
(91)	330–335 / 805–810	1/3 Pepys Street and Savage Gardens	13.1.72 C	Offices	13·7	9–10	(L) & (T)	Little recorded in area. Unknown	(Unknown)	(Part of precinct of Crutched Friars)

Development probable in next five years

125	335–340 / 810–815	Area S. of India Street, Crutched Friars and Minories, to railway	—	Outstanding from L.C.C. Development Plan 1962	13·7–15·2	9·1–10·7	(L) & (T)	Ditch and length of city wall at 1 Crutched Friars. Cemetery? Occupation?	Site crosses line of city wall. Occupation? Ditch?	City wall and ditch. Occupation?
126	—	13/15 Cooper's Row	—	Outstanding from L.C.C. Development Plan 1962	13·1	9·1–10·7	(L)	Little recorded in area. Unknown	Unknown	Occupation

335–340/810–815

Development imminent

127	—	11/18 Houndsditch, 22/30 Duke's Place	ODP 6.1.72	—	15·8	>10·7	(L) & (P)	City wall and ditches	City wall and ditch	City wall, ditch and bastion
	—	2/9 Houndsditch, 4/22 Duke's Place	—	Approved						
128	—	7/18 Aldgate High Street, 11/15 St Botolph's Row	ODP 21.2.70	Scheme under consideration	16·2	>10·7	(L)	Beyond city wall and Aldgate. Suburban development? Cemetery?	Suburban occupation?	Suburban occupation

(1) Ref. no.	(2) Other 500 m squares	(3) Address of site	(4) Date of planning permission	(5) Proposed development	(6) Approx. present land surface	(7) Approx. Roman land surface	(8) Probable basement destruction	(9) Archaeological Potential Roman c.A.D.43–c.450	(10) Archaeological Potential Anglo-Saxon c.450–1066	(11) Archaeological Potential Medieval 1066–c.1500
					In metres above O.D.					
129	—	3/6 Jewry Street, Sir John Cass College	1.6.61	Public building	14·0	9–10	—	Little recorded in area. Occupation? To S. of site of early fort ditch	Unknown. Occupation on Saxon intra-mural street?	Occupation
Development probable in next five years										
130	—	Site bounded by Aldgate High Street and Minories	—	Part of Gardiner's Corner proposed G.L.C. and L.B. mixed development area	15·2	9–11	(L), (P) & (T)	N. of Goodman Fields burial area. Cemetery and/or suburban development	Probable occupation on early frontage of Aldgate High Street	Suburban occupation
131	—	84/89 Aldgate High Street, 155/157 Minories, 36/37 Jewry Street	—	Outstanding from L.C.C. Development Plan 1962	15·9	>10	(L) & (P)	On line of city wall, still preserved at 36 Jewry Street. Ditches	On city wall near Aldgate. Ditch	(On city wall near Aldgate. Ditch)
(125)	335–340 805–810	Area S. of India Street, Crutched Friars and Minories, to railway	—	Outstanding from L.C.C. Development Plan 1962	13·7– 15·2	9·1– 10·7	(L) & (T)	Ditch and length of city wall at 1 Crutched Friars. Cemetery? Occupation?	Site crosses line of city wall. Occupation? Ditch?	City wall and ditch. Occupation?

Appendix II

The sources of maps 1–8 and figures 1–9

Maps in the case

Map 1 Base map: the City and County of the City of London

Reproduced and reduced from the 1:2500 Ordnance Survey Map, with the sanction of the Controller of H.M. Stationery Office.

Map 2 Roman London, c.A.D.43 – c.450

Based on *3*. Merrifield 1965 with its folding map and gazetteer; *2*. RCHM 1928; *3*. Merrifield 1969; *11*. Dawe and Oswald 1952; *11*. Grimes 1968. Excavation sites not covered in *3*. Merrifield 1965 were added from the following journals (see Appendix III, Bibliography, Section 3, for full details): *Transactions of the London and Middlesex Archaeological Society* 8–11 and n.s. 18–23 (1940–71); *Archaeological News Letter* 1.1 – 7.9 (April 1948 – February 1965); *Current Archaeology* 1–33 (March 1967 – July 1972); *The London Archaeologist* 1.1 – 1.15 (Winter 1968 – July 1972); *Journal of Roman Studies* 53 – 9 (1963–9); *Britannia* 1 – 2 (1970–1). Additional information on unpublished excavations was provided by the staff of Guildhall Museum from their *Excavation Register*.

Map 3 Anglo-Saxon London, c.450–1066

Based on *4*. Wheeler 1935; *5*. Baker 1970; *11*. Grimes 1968; and the following journals (see Appendix III, Bibliography, Section 4, for full details): *Trans. London Middlesex Archaeol. Soc*; *Archaeol. News Letter*; *Medieval Archaeol.* 1 – 15 (1957–71). Find-spots subsequent to *4*. Wheeler 1935 were added from Guildhall Museum records, and from *4*. Wilson 1964. Finds of sub-Roman 'B' ware were included; also finds of Badorf ware, but not finds of Pingsdorf ware. Individual coin finds were not included, nor find-spots which were very uncertain. Coin-hoards, where the provenance was sufficiently precise, were added from *13*. Thompson 1956, and *13*. Dolley 1960. Early street-names were taken from *7*. Ekwall 1954. Information about churches and church dedications was kindly provided by Professor C. N. L. Brooke and Mrs G. Keir, both of Westfield College, University of London. The lines of the watercourses are from *3*. Merrifield 1965; the waterfront is only approximate.

Map 4 Medieval London, 1066–c.1500

The most valuable works of reference for this map were *2*. Harben 1919, *7*. Ekwall 1954, *8*. Honeybourne 1960. Additional information was provided by Guildhall Museum. The company halls were taken from the map in *2*. Holden and Holford 1951, 130. Information on excavations was taken from *11*. Grimes 1968 and from the following journals (see

Appendix III, Bibliography, Section 5, for full details): *Trans. London Middlesex Archaeol. Soc., Archaeol. News Letter, Medieval Archaeol.* An extensive number of observations were added from Guildhall Museum's *Excavation Register*.

Map 5 Modern London: depth of basements

The main source for this map is the series of insurance plans for the City of London compiled by Messrs Chas. Goad Ltd, and revised by them to 1969–70 (these plans are no longer kept up to date). The lines of cut-and-cover railway lines were added from information supplied by Guildhall Museum and from the map of nineteenth-century underground railways in *2*. Holden and Holford 1951, 165.

Map 6 London: depth of archaeological deposits

The source for this map was the contour-map accompanying *3*. Marsden 1972, 840. Depths of archaeological deposits were taken from excavation reports in *3*. Merrifield 1965, *11*. Grimes 1968, and *Trans. London Middlesex Archaeol. Soc.* (see Appendix III, Bibliography, Sections 3, 4, and 5).

Map 7 London: age of buildings, listed buildings, public and private open spaces

Information on open spaces is from Corporation of London, Department of Architecture and Planning, *Map of open spaces,* based on an open space survey of 1968, with some additions and omissions. Age of buildings is taken from *9*. Corporation of London 1968 (note that this map excludes the Temple). Listed buildings are from the statutory and supplementary lists prepared by the Department of the Environment. Development information is from: Corporation of London, *Progress of Rebuilding,* a list produced every year and quarterly (the following lists were used: position as at 31.12.69; position as at 31.12.71; position as at 30.6.72; position as at 30.9.72); Corporation of London, *Summary of Office Development Permissions,* 1965–70; *Office Development Permissions for development and extensions* as at 31.3.72. Other sources: *9*. Corporation of London 1969; *9*. Corporation of London 1966; *9*. Corporation of London (n.d.); *9*. Corporation of London 1960. Road proposals included in this map from information provided by the Corporation of London, City Engineer's Department.

Map 8 London: the extent of future destruction

Conservation areas were taken from Corporation of London, Department of Architecture and Planning, *Map of Conservation Areas.* Other sources are the same as those for Map 7. Study areas are taken from information provided by the Corporation of London, Department of Architecture and Planning. Note that study areas are those areas where a survey of the possible problems involved in redevelopment has been undertaken, but that the areas are not necessarily to be redeveloped. Also included in this map were areas to be redeveloped still outstanding from the London County Council *Development Plan* of 1962 (slightly amended).

Figures in the text

Figure 1 Areas of the City destroyed by enemy action, 1939–45
Taken from maps in 2. Holden and Holford 1951.

Figures 2, 3a, and 3b. London and some other medieval walled towns in England and elsewhere in Europe
The plans for these figures were taken from books and journals too numerous to quote, but F. Ganshof, *Etude sur le développement des villes d'entre Loire et Rhin au moyen âge* (Paris 1943) was especially useful.

Figure 4 Archaeology in the City: the emphasis of research
Compiled from Maps 2, 3, and 4, substituting a black dot for *all* symbols representing archaeological excavation or observation.

Figure 5 The depth of archaeological deposits in the City: a summary
Compiled from Map 6, augmented by information from Guildhall Museum.

Figure 6 The state of archaeological deposits in the City: a summary
Compiled from Map 5, simplified.

Figure 7 The state of archaeological deposits in the City: sample areas
Compiled from Maps 2, 5, and 8. Partial destruction of archaeological levels is assumed below modern streets.

Figure 8 The future of archaeological deposits in the City: a summary
Compiled from Map 8.

Figure 9 The development of London
This series of maps is intended to represent in sketch form some idea of London's development between A.D.43 and the end of the sixteenth century. Some aspects are inevitably conjectural. The sketches were compiled in general from Maps 2, 3, and 4, with additional information from Guildhall Museum; and the Cuming Museum, Southwark. The red stipple on *fig.9.6, c.1570*, is based on the built-up area shown on Braun and Hogenberg's map of London 1572.

Appendix III

The archaeology of the City: a select bibliography

Compiled by Carolyn M. Heighway

This bibliography is not intended to be a comprehensive list of the very great number of works on the history and archaeology of London. It is intended as an outline summary of useful works of scholarship, particularly those which have formed the basis of this study. All works cited in the text are preceded by a numerical prefix representing the section of this bibliography in which that work will be found. The Borough of Southwark and City of Westminster have not been included in detail, although a few general works relating to Southwark have been included at the end of Sections 2, 10e, and 11. The place of publication is London, unless otherwise stated.

1 BIBLIOGRAPHICAL WORKS

A list of bibliographical works relating to the City of London in general. For bibliographies of the Roman, Saxon, medieval, and early modern periods, see Sections 3, 4, 5, and 6 respectively.

Works in other sections containing useful bibliographical material are marked with an asterisk.

CBA, 1940. Council for British Archaeology, *Archaeological Bibliography* (annual publication, covering period 1940 onwards).

GODFREY, 1942. W. H. Godfrey, 'Philip Norman, 1842–1931. Also a list of his works relating to London', *London Topographical Record*, 17 (1942), 140–56.

GROSS, 1966. C. Gross, *A Bibliography of British Municipal History* (1st edn, 1897; 2nd edn, 1966, with preface by G. H. Martin).
Section on London, 286–325.

GUILDHALL LIBRARY, 1959. Guildhall Library, *The County of London: a select book list* (1959).

GUILDHALL MUSEUM, 1908. Guildhall Museum, *Catalogue of the collection of London Antiquities* (2nd edn, 1908).

HISTORICAL ASSOCIATION. *Annual Bulletin of Historical Literature* (1911 onwards).

JONES AND SMITH, 1951. P. E. Jones and R. Smith, *A Guide to the records in the Corporation of London Records Office and the Guildhall Library Muniment Room* (1951).

MARTIN AND MACINTYRE, 1972. G. H. Martin and S. MacIntyre, *A Bibliography of British and Irish Municipal History 1: General Works* (Leicester 1972).
Brings *1*. Gross 1966 up-to-date by including works 1897–1966.

NATIONAL BOOK LEAGUE, 1971. *London and its environs* [a booklist] (1971).

RUBENSTEIN, 1968. S. Rubenstein, *Historians of London: an account of the many surveys, histories, perambulations, maps and engravings made about the City and its environs and of the dedicated Londoners who made them* (1968).

SIMS, 1970. J. M. Sims, *London and Middlesex published records: a handlist* (London Record Society 1970).

SMITH, 1951. R. Smith, *The City of London – a select booklist* (1951).

V AND A, 1964. Victoria and Albert Museum, *The growth of London AD 43 – 1964: catalogue of an exhibition at the museum, 17 July – 30 August 1964* (1964).

2 GENERAL HISTORICAL AND TOPOGRAPHICAL WORKS

Historical

BROOKE, 1968. C. N. L. Brooke, *Time, the Arch-satirist: an inaugural lecture delivered at Westfield College (University of London) 1968* (1968).

HOLDEN AND HOLFORD, 1951. C. H. Holden and W. G. Holford, *The City of London: a record of destruction and survival* (1951).

*HOLLAENDER AND KELLAWAY, 1969. A. E. J. Hollaender and W. Kellaway, *Studies in London History presented to Philip Edmund Jones* (1969).

PAGE, 1923. W. Page, *London: its origin and early development* (1923).
Out of date in some respects but not yet superseded.

SHARPE, 1894–5. R. R. Sharpe, *London and the Kingdom* (3 volumes, 1894–5).
Still the standard political work on London.

VCH LONDON, 1909. W. Page (ed.), *Victoria History of the County of London*, I (1909).

Topographical

HARBEN, 1919. H. A. Harben, *A Dictionary of London* (1919).
The best historical–topographical dictionary of the city.

*KENT, 1951. W. Kent (ed.), *An Encyclopaedia of London* (1951).

LONDON SURVEY, 1924, 1929, 1934. F. Shepherd (ed.), *Survey of London*, 9 (1924), 12 (1929), 15 (1934).
These are the only volumes concerning City parishes.

PEVSNER, 1957. N. Pevsner, *London 1: The Cities of London and Westminster* (Buildings of England, 11, 1957).

RCHM, 1924, 1925, 1928, 1929, 1930. Royal Commission on Historical Monuments (England), *An inventory of the historical monuments in London* (5 volumes: 1 Westminster Abbey (1924); 2 West London (1925); 3 Roman London (1928); 4 The City (1929); 5 East London (1930)).

STOW, 1908. John Stow (ed. Charles L. Kingsford), *A Survey of London 1603* (2 volumes, Oxford 1908).

WHEATLEY, 1891. H. B. Wheatley, *London Past and Present: its history, associations and traditions* (3 volumes, 1891).
Useful topographical reference work.

Southwark

JOHNSON, 1969. D. J. Johnson, *Southwark and the City* (Oxford 1969).

MANNING AND BRAY, 1814. O. Manning and W. Bray, *History and Antiquities of Surrey*, III (1814), 545ff.

VCH SURREY, 1911. H. Malden (ed.), *Victoria History of the County of Surrey*, IV (1911), 125ff.

Local Journals and Publications

Guildhall Miscellany (*Guildhall Misc.*).
Journal of the London Society (*J. London Soc.*).
London Archaeologist (*London Archaeol.*).
London Record Society Publications (LRS).
London Topographical Record (*LTR*).
London Topographical Society Publications (LTS).
Transactions of the London and Middlesex Archaeological Society (*Trans. London Middlesex Archaeol. Soc.*).

3 ROMAN LONDON
Bibliographical works

There is a good bibliography of Roman London in *3*. Merrifield 1965, 327 – 32. Only material published in 1965 and later is therefore included in this bibliography, except where specific references are needed to support statements in the text. For recent information on finds and excavations in Roman London, see *3*. Wilson 1965–72, and *11*. Marsden 1967–71.

BONSER, 1957. W. Bonser, *A Romano-British Bibliography 55 BC – AD 449* (2 volumes, Oxford 1957).

Other works

CELORIA, 1965. F. Celoria, 'Archaeological finds from the Counties of London and Middlesex added to the Collections of the London Museum during 1962', *Trans. London Middlesex Archaeol. Soc.*, 21.2 (1965), 140–1.

DUNNING, 1945. G. C. Dunning, 'Two Fires of Roman London', *Antiq. J.*, 25 (1945), 45–77.

GRIMES, 1968. See *11*. Grimes 1968.

LAMBERT, 1915. F. Lambert, 'Recent Roman Discoveries in London', *Archaeologia*, 66 (1915), 225–74.

MARSDEN, 1967a. See *11*. Marsden 1967.

MARSDEN, 1967b. P. R. V. Marsden, *A Ship of the Roman Period, from Blackfriars, in the City of London* (Guildhall Museum, n.d. [1967]).

MARSDEN, 1968a. P. R. V. Marsden, 'Roman house and bath at Billingsgate', *London Archaeol.*, 1 (1968), 3–5.

MARSDEN, 1968b. See *11*. Marsden 1968.

MARSDEN, 1969a. P. R. V. Marsden, 'The Roman pottery industry of London', *Trans. London Middlesex Archaeol. Soc.*, 22.2 (1969), 39–44.

MARSDEN, 1969b. See *11*. Marsden 1969.

MARSDEN, 1969c. P. R. V. Marsden, 'Excavation of a Roman public bath', *London Archaeol.*, 1.5 (1969), 108–10.

MARSDEN, 1970. See *11*. Marsden 1970.

MARSDEN, 1971. See *11*. Marsden 1971.

MARSDEN, 1972. P. R. V. Marsden, 'Mapping the birth of Londinium', *Geographical Magazine*, 44.12 (1972), 840–5.

MERRIFIELD, 1965. R. Merrifield, *The Roman City of London* (1965).

MERRIFIELD, 1967. R. Merrifield, 'Old Bailey Extension', *Kent Archaeol. Rev.*, 9 (1967), 14.

MERRIFIELD, 1969. R. Merrifield, *Roman London* (1969).

PHILP, 1969. B. Philp, 'Emergency excavations in the Forum area', *London Archaeol.*, 1.2 (1969) 36–7.

PRYCE AND OSWALD, 1928. T. Davies Pryce and F. Oswald, 'Roman London: Its initial occupation as evidenced by early types of Terra Sigillata', *Archaeologia*, 78 (1928), 73–110.

RCHM, 1928. See *2*. RCHM 1928.

RODWELL, 1972. Warwick Rodwell, *Roman London, its roads and the Antonine Itinerary* (unpublished thesis, Institute of Archaeology, University of London, 1972).

SPENCER, 1967. B. W. Spencer, 'Archaeological finds from the Counties of London and Middlesex added to the collections of the London Museum 1963–4', *Trans. London Middlesex Archaeol. Soc.*, 21.3 (1967) 222–3.

WILSON, 1965–72. D. R. Wilson, 'Roman Britain in 1964/1965/1966/1967/1968/1969/1970/1971', *J. Roman Stud.* 55 (1965), 214–5; *ibid.*, 56 (1966), 210–11; *ibid.*, 57 (1967), 191–2; *ibid.*, 58 (1968), 197; *ibid.*, 59 (1969), 224; *Britannia* 1 (1970), 292; *ibid.*, 2 (1971), 274; *ibid.*, 3 (1972), 335.

4 ANGLO-SAXON LONDON
Bibliographical works

BONSER, 1957. W. Bonser, *An Anglo-Saxon and Celtic Bibliography AD 450–1087* (Oxford 1957).

Other works

BAILEY, 1972. K. Bailey, 'Saxon settlements south of the Thames – some further observations', *London Archaeol.*, 1.14 (1972), 328–9.

BIDDLE AND HILL, 1971. Martin Biddle and David Hill, 'Late Saxon Planned Towns', *Antiq. J.*, 51 (1971) 70–85.

BIRCH, 1888. W. de G. Birch, 'The early notices of the Danes in England to the Battle of Brunanburgh, AD 937, and the rebuilding of the city of London by King Alfred, AD 886', *J. Brit. Archaeol. Assoc.*, 44 (1888), 326–42.

COOK, 1969a. N. C. Cook, 'An Anglo-Saxon saucer brooch from Lower Thames Street, London', *Antiq. J.*, 49.2 (1969), 1–9.

COOK 1969b. N. C. Cook, 'A fifth century wheel-made sherd from the City of London', *Antiq. J.* 49.2 (1969), 396.

DUNNING, MYRES, AND TISCHLER, 1959. G. C. Dunning, J. N. L. Myres, and F. Tischler, 'Anglo-Saxon pottery: a symposium', *Medieval Archaeol.*, 3 (1959), 1–78. Includes local and imported pottery from London.

EMINSON, 1932. T. B. F. Eminson, *Saxon London and its Knightengild* (Gainsborough 1932).

GOMME, 1912. Sir G. L. Gomme, *The Making of London* (Oxford 1912).

GRIMES, 1968. See *11*. Grimes 1968.

HONEYBOURNE, 1933. M. B. Honeybourne, 'The Sanctuary Boundaries and Environs of Westminster Abbey and the College of St. Martin-le-Grand', *J. Brit. Archaeol. Ass.*, 2nd s., 38 (1933), 316–33.

LETHABY, 1902. W. R. Lethaby, *London before the Conquest* (1902).

LETHABY, 1907. W. R. Lethaby, *London before the Conqueror* (1907).

MARSDEN, 1963. P. R. V. Marsden, 'Ancient ships in London', *Mariner's Mirror*, 49.2 (1963), 144–5.

MARSDEN, 1967. See *11*. Marsden, 1967. Anglo-Saxon finds in the city.

MARSDEN, 1968. P. R. V. Marsden, 'Some discoveries in the City of London, 1954–9', *Trans. London Middlesex Archaeol. Soc.*, 22.1 (1968), 32–42.
Find of Saxon bone comb.

MYRES, 1934. J. N. L. Myres, 'Some thoughts on the topography of Saxon London', *Antiquity*, 8 (1934), 437–42.
A reply to *4*. Wheeler 1934a.

OSWALD, 1948. A. Oswald, 'A bronze Viking drinking horn from Fetter Lane, London', *Antiq. J.*, 28 (1948), 179.

OSWALD, 1949. See *11*. Oswald 1949.
Dark-age finds. See also *J. Roman. Stud.*, 39 (1949), 107.

PAGE, 1919. W. Page, 'Notes on some early riverside settlements of London', *Proc. Soc. Antiq.*, 2nd s., 31 (1919), 125–7.

SMEDLEY AND OWLES, 1965. N. Smedley and E. Owles, 'Some Anglo-Saxon "animal" brooches', *Proc. Suffolk. Inst. Archaeol.*, 30.2 (1965), 166–74.
Includes Cheapside disc brooch.

SMITH, 1909. R. A. Smith, 'Anglo-Saxon remains [of London]', see *2*. VCH London 1909, 147–70.

SMITH, 1917. R. A. Smith, 'Roman roads and the distribution of Saxon churches in London', *Archaeologia*, 68 (1917), 229–62.

SPENCER, 1967. See *3*. Spencer 1967.
Scramasax from the City.

TITFORD, 1971. C. Titford, 'Saxon Settlements South of the Thames', *London Archaeol.*, 1.13 (1971), 296–7.

WATERMAN, 1959. D. M. Waterman, 'Late Saxon, Viking and Early Medieval Finds from York', *Archaeologia*, 97 (1959), 59–105.
London finds mentioned.

WHEELER, 1927. R. E. M. Wheeler (Sir Mortimer), *London and the Vikings* (London Museum Catalogues 1, 1927).

WHEELER, 1934a. R. E. M. Wheeler (Sir Mortimer), 'The Topography of Saxon London', *Antiquity*, 8 (1934), 290–302, 443–47.

WHEELER, 1934b. R. E. M. Wheeler (Sir Mortimer), 'London and the Grim's ditches', *Antiq. J.*, 14 (1934) 254–63.

WHEELER, 1935. R. E. M. Wheeler (Sir Mortimer), *London and the Saxons* (London Museum Catalogues 6, 1935).

WHITELOCK, 1955. Dorothy Whitelock (ed), *English Historical Documents, c.500–1042* (1955).

WILSON, 1964. D. M. Wilson, *Anglo-Saxon Ornamental Metalwork, 700–1100, in the British Museum* (1964).

WILSON AND HURST, 1960–70. D. M. Wilson and D. G. Hurst, 'Medieval Britain in 1959/1960/1969', *Medieval Archaeol.*, 4 (1960) 136; *ibid.*, 5 (1961), 309; *ibid.*, 14 (1970). 161.
Other London Anglo-Saxon finds, see: *Trans. London Middlesex Archaeol. Soc.*, 21.1 (1962), 78; *ibid.*, 21.2 (1965), 139; *Illustrated London News* (2.8.47), 135.

5 MEDIEVAL LONDON

Only the most important topographical and historical works for the medieval period have been cited here. Many detailed articles on individual buildings, architecture, etc. can be extracted from the CBA Archaeological Bibliography (*1*. CBA 1940).

Apart from Professor Grimes' work, there were few important excavations of medieval levels in London before 1957, the year when excavation summaries began to appear in *Medieval Archaeology* (*5*. Hurst 1960–9), but see *11*. Grimes 1968 and *5*. Knowles and Grimes 1954.

Most books and articles on the extensive written sources of medieval London are not included. For a selection of these, refer to *1*. Gross 1966, *1*. Martin and MacIntyre 1972 and *1*. Smith 1951.

Bibliographical works and catalogues

LONDON MUSEUM, 1967. London Museum, *Medieval Catalogue* (repr. 1967).

Other works

BAKER, 1970. T. Baker, *Medieval London* (1970).

COLVIN, 1963. H. M. Colvin (ed.), *The History of the King's Works:* I and II, *The Middle Ages* (1963).
Tower of London, II, 706–29.

DARBY AND CAMPBELL, 1962. H. C. Darby and E. M. J. Campbell, *The Domesday Geography of South-East England* (Cambridge 1962).
Middlesex, 97–137.

DOUGLAS AND GREENAWAY, 1953. D. C. Douglas and G. W. Greenaway (eds), *English Historical Documents 1042–1189* (1953).
pp. 944–62: select documents relating to London.

EKWALL, 1956. E. Ekwall, *Studies on the Population of Medieval London* (Stockholm 1956).

GUILDHALL MUSEUM, 1961. See *11*. Guildhall 1961.

HARRIS, 1958. E. Harris, 'A medieval undercroft at 50 Mark Lane, London E.C.3', *Medieval Archaeol.*, 2 (1958), 178–82.

HONEYBOURNE, 1966. M. B. Honeybourne, 'Norman London', *London and Middlesex Historian*, 3 (1966), 9–14.

HURST, 1960, 1964, 1965, 1966, 1969. D. G. Hurst, 'Medieval Britain in 1959/1962–3/1964/1966/1968/', *Medieval Archaeol.*, 4 (1960), 149; *ibid.*, 8 (1964), 255; *ibid.*, 9 (1965), 179–220; *ibid.*, 11 (1967), 294; *ibid.*, 13 (1969), 251, 265.

KNOWLES AND GRIMES, 1954. M. D. Knowles and W. F. Grimes, *Charterhouse: the medieval foundation in the light of recent discoveries* (1954).

MARSDEN, 1967–71. See *11*. Marsden 1967, 1968, 1969, 1970, 1971.

MORTON AND MUNTZ, 1972. Catherine Morton and Hope Muntz (eds), *Carmen de Hastingae Proelio* (Oxford 1972)
Especially lines 635ff, and notes.

★MYERS, 1972. A. R. Myers, *London in the Age of Chaucer* (Oklahoma 1972).

REID, 1954. K. C. Reid, 'The Water-Mills of London', *Trans. London Middlesex Archaeol. Soc.*, 11.3 (1954), 227–36.

STENTON, 1915. F. M. Stenton, *Norman London* (Historical Association pamphlet 38, 1915).

STENTON, 1934. F. M. Stenton, *Norman London* (Historical Association pamphlet 93–4, 1934).
Revised and enlarged from *5*. Stenton 1915.

STENTON, 1960. F. M. Stenton, 'Norman London', *Social Life in Early England* (ed. G. Barraclough 1960), 179–207.
Again re-written and revised from *5*. Stenton 1934. Reprinted again in *Preparatory to Anglo-Saxon England* (ed. D. M. Stenton, Oxford 1970).

THRUPP, 1962. Sylvia A. Thrupp, *The Merchant Class of Medieval London* (Ann Arbor 1962).

★WILLIAMS, 1963. G. A. Williams, *From Commune to Capital* (1963).

6 EARLY MODERN LONDON

Bibliographical works and catalogues

See *1*. Gross 1966, *1*. Martin and MacIntyre 1972 and *1*. Smith 1951.

LONDON MUSEUM, 1966. London Museum, *Dated Post-medieval Pottery in the London Museum* (1966).

Other works

BRETT-JAMES, 1935. N. G. Brett-James, *The Growth of Stuart London* (1935).

CHANCELLOR, 1907. E. B. Chancellor, *The History of the Squares of London, Topographical and Historical etc.* (1907).

DAVIS, 1924. E. J. Davis, 'The Transformation of London', *Tudor Studies presented . . . to Albert Frederick Pollard* (ed. R. W. Seton-Watson 1924), 287–314.

GEORGE, 1966. D. George, *London Life in the Eighteenth Century* (rev. edn, 1966).

HOBHOUSE, 1971. Hermione Hobhouse, *Lost London: a century of demolition and decay* (1971).

MOORHOUSE, 1967–72. S. Moorhouse, 'Post-Medieval Britain in 1966/1967/1968/1970/1971', *Post-Medieval Archaeol.*, 1 (1967), 115; *ibid.*, 2 (1968), 180; 3 (1969), 193, 195, 196, 199, 204; *ibid.*, 5 (1971), 207, 212; *ibid.*, 6 (1972), 211.

OLSON, 1964. See 9. Olson 1964.

REDDAWAY, 1940. T. F. Reddaway, *The Rebuilding of London after the Great Fire* (1940).

SUMMERSON, 1962. Sir John Summerson, *Georgian London* (rev. edn, 1970).

7 PLACE AND PERSONAL NAMES

BOHMAN, 1944. Hjordis Bohman, *Studies in the Middle English dialects of Devon and London* (Göteborg 1944).

BONNER, 1917. A. Bonner, 'Some London Street-Names: their antiquity and origin', *Trans. London and Middlesex Archaeol. Soc.*, n.s., 3 (1917), 185–216; 287–320.

EKWALL, 1945. E. Ekwall, *Variation in Surnames in Medieval London* (Lund 1945).

EKWALL, 1947. E. Ekwall, *Early London Personal Names* (Lund 1947).

*EKWALL, 1954. E. Ekwall, *Street-Names of the City of London* (Oxford 1954).

GOVER, 1922. J. E. B. Gover, *The Place-Names of Middlesex* (1922).

HARBEN, 1896. F. H. Harben, *London Street-Names: their origin, signification, and historic value: with divers notes and observations* (1896).

MACKENZIE, 1928. B. A. Mackenzie, *The Early London Dialect* (Oxford 1928).

RAWLINGS, 1926. G. B. Rawlings, *The Streets of London, their history and associations* (1926).

RUMBLE [1972]. A. Rumble, *Bibliography for a Survey of the Place-Names of the City of London* (English Place-Name Soc., London Univ., unpublished, n.d. [1972]).

STEVENSON, 1888. W. H. Stevenson, 'Danish Place-names around London', *Academy*, 33 (1888) 189–90.

TAIT, 1931. J. Tait, 'Unknown names of early London wards', *LTR*, 15 (1931), 1–3.

ZETTERSTEIN, 1926. L. Zetterstein, *City Street-Names* (3rd edition, 1926).

8 MAPS

BODLEIAN, 1960. Bodleian Library, *The Large Scale County Maps of the British Isles 1596–1850, a Union List* (Oxford 1960).

CRACE, 1878. J. G. Crace (ed.), *A catalogue of maps, plans and drawings of London, Westminster and Southwark* (1878).

DARLINGTON AND HOWGEGO, 1964. I. Darlington and J. Howgego, *Printed maps of London circa 1553–1850* (1964).

GLANVILLE, 1972. P. Glanville, *London in Maps* (1972).

HOLMES, 1958. M. Holmes, 'London on the Map', *Museums J.*, 58.4 (1958), 75–7.

HOLMES, 1966. M. Holmes, 'An unrecorded map of London', *Archaeologia*, 100 (1966), 105–128.

HONEYBOURNE, 1960. M. B. Honeybourne, *A sketch map of London under Richard II* (LTS Publication no. 93, 1960). Review in *Geogr. J.*, 127 (1961), 127.

HONEYBOURNE, 1965. M. B. Honeybourne, 'The Reconstructed Map of London under Richard II', *LTR*, 22 (1965), 29–76.

HURSTFIELD AND SKELTON, 1965. J. Hurstfield and R. A. Skelton, 'John Norden's View of London 1600', *LTR*, 22 (1965), 5–28.

MARKS, 1964. S. P. Marks, *The Map of Mid-Sixteenth Century London* (LTS Publication no. 100, 1964).

SCOULOUDI, 1955. I. Scouloudi, 'A discovery at the Public Record Office', *Guildhall Misc.*, 4 (1955), 36–7.

STENTON, 1934. F. M. Stenton, 'A sketch map of London under Henry II', in 5. Stenton 1934.

9 PLANNING

Reference should also be made to the sources used for Map 7 listed in Appendix II, p.75.

BOOKER AND GREEN, 1973. Christopher Booker and Candida Lycett Green, *Goodbye London: An Illustrated Guide to Threatened Buildings* (1973)

CEMENT AND CONCRETE, 1971. Cement and Concrete Association, *Barbican* (1971).

CORPORATION OF LONDON, n.d. Corporation of London, *The Barbican Residential Development* (n.d.).

CORPORATION OF LONDON, 1960. Corporation of London, *The Tower of London Precinct* (1960).

CORPORATION OF LONDON, 1966. Corporation of London, *The Guildhall Development* (1966)

CORPORATION OF LONDON, 1968. Corporation of London, Architecture and Planning Department, *Age of Buildings Survey Map* (1.9.1968).

CORPORATION OF LONDON, 1969. Corporation of London; E. G. Chandler, City Architect and Planning Officer, *Redevelopment Proposals for the North Bank Area in the City of London* (February 1969).

DEPARTMENT OF THE ENVIROMENT, 1972. Department of the Environment, *List of Buildings of Special Architectural or Historic Interest: City of London* (June 1972).

DUNNING, 1969. J. H. Dunning, 'The City of London: A Case Study in Urban Economics', *Town Planning Review*, 40.3 (1969).

DUNNING AND MORGAN, 1971. J. H. Dunning and E. V. Morgan, *An Economic Study of the City of London* (1971).

GLC, 1966–70. Greater London Council, Dept. of Planning and Transportation, *Annual Abstract of Greater London Statistics* (1966–70).

GLC, 1969a. Greater London Council, *Greater London Development Plan: Statement* (1969).

GLC, 1969b. Greater London Council, *Greater London Development Plan: Report of Studies* (1969).

GLC, 1972. Greater London Council, Department of Planning and Transportation, *The Land Use Survey* (Research Report no. 8, 1972).

HEIGHWAY, 1972. C. M. Heighway (ed.), *The Erosion of History: Archaeology and Planning in Towns* (Council for British Archaeology, 1972).

HOLFORD, 1966. W. G. Holford (Lord Holford), 'Reconstruction in the City of London: a review by Lord Holford of 20 years' work', *Building* (22 July 1966).

HOLFORD, 1968. W. G. Holford (Lord Holford), *Report to the Common Council of the Corporation of London on the area South and West of St. Paul's Cathedral in the City of London* (1968).

OLSON, 1964. D. J. Olson, *Town Planning in London: the eighteenth and nineteenth centuries* (Yale 1964).

SCOTT, 1966. Sir G. Scott and Partners, *Guildhall Precincts Report* (1966).

WHEELER, 1944. R. E. M. Wheeler (Sir Mortimer), 'The Rebuilding of London', *Antiquity*, 18 (1944), 151–2.

10 TOPOGRAPHY

10a Site

AKEROYD, 1972. A. V. Akeroyd, 'Archaeological and historical evidence for subsidence in South Britain', in K. C. Dunham and D. A. Gray, 'A discussion on problems associated with the subsidence of South-East England', *Phil. Trans. Roy. Soc. London.*, A 272 (1972), 151–69.

*BARTON, 1962. N. J. Barton, *The Lost Rivers of London: a study of their effects upon London and Londoners, and the effects of London and Londoners upon them* (1962).

CLAYTON, 1964. R. Clayton (ed.), *The Geography of Greater London: a source book for teacher and student* (1964).

CODRINGTON, 1915. T. Codrington, 'London South of the Thames', *Surrey Archaeol. Collect.*, 28 (1915) 111–63.

GOMME, 1909–10. G. L. Gomme, 'The Geography of early London', *Geographical Teacher*, 5 (1909–10), 321–34.

RAYNS, 1971. A. W. Rayns, *The London Region* (1971).

SHERLOCK, 1960. R. L. Sherlock, *London and the Thames Valley* (British Regional Geology Series, 3rd edn, 1960).

10b Defences

BELL, 1937. W. G. Bell *et al., London Wall through eighteen centuries* (1937).

FORTY, 1955. F. J. Forty, 'London wall by St. Alphage's churchyard: exposure and presentation of Roman and medieval work in the Town Wall of London', *Guildhall Misc.*, 5 (1955) 4–59.

FORTY, 1956. F. J. Forty, 'The Ancient wall of the City of London', *J. London Soc.*, 333 (1956), 23–33.

HUGHES, 1955. E. H. Hughes, *The Gates of London* (1955).

MARSDEN, 1967. P. R. V. Marsden, 'The Riverside defensive wall of Roman London', *Trans. London Middlesex Archaeol. Soc.*, 21 (1967) 149–56.

10c Street Plan

There is a paucity of works on the street plan of the City of London.

For the streets, see *2*. Harben 1918, *7*. Ekwall 1954, and also:

HASLAM, 1972. Jeremy Haslam, 'Medieval Streets in London', *London Archaeol.*, 2.1 (1972), 3–7.

HONEYBOURNE, 1971. M. B. Honeybourne, 'The City of London's Historic Streets', *Trans. Ancient Monuments Soc.*, n.s., 18 (1971), 77–93.

10d Bridge

DAVIDGE, 1952. W. R. Davidge, 'The Bridges of London', *J. London Soc.*, 314 (1952), 136–43.

DAWSON, 1969. G. Dawson, 'Roman London Bridge', *London Archaeol.*, 1.5 (1969), 114–7.

DAWSON, 1970. G. Dawson, 'Roman London Bridge. Part 2: Its location', *London Archaeol.*, 1.7 (1970), 156–60.

DAWSON, 1971a. G. Dawson, 'London Bridge – a rejoinder', *London Archaeol.*, 1.10 (1971), 224.

DAWSON, 1971b. G. Dawson, 'Comment on Tooley St., Southwark, excavations in so far as they relate to the position of the Saxon bridge', *London Archaeol.*, 1.11 (1971), 254.

DAWSON, 1972. G. Dawson, 'The Saxon London Bridge', *London Archaeol.*, 1.14 (1972), 330–2.

HOME, 1931. G. C. Home, *Old London Bridge* (1931).

HONEYBOURNE, 1969. M. B. Honeybourne, 'The Pre-Norman Bridge of London', in *2*. Hollaender and Kellaway 1969.

MERRIFIELD, 1970. R. Merrifield, 'Roman London Bridge: Further Observations on its Site', *London Archaeol.*, 1.8 (1970) 186–7.

10e Churches

Very little reliable work has been done on London churches in general. There are numerous short articles in journals concerning individual churches, but many of these are now out-of-date.

The following general works may be of use:

Bibliographical works

SMITH, 1951. See *1*. Smith 1951, 10–13, 'Religion'.

Other works

BROOKE, 1970. C. N. L. Brooke, 'The Missionary at Home: The Church in the Towns 1000–1250', *Studies in Church History, 6 The Mission of the Church and Propagation of the Faith* (ed. G. Cuming, Cambridge 1970).

CLARKE, 1966. B. F. L. Clarke, *The Parish Churches of London* (1966).

COBB, 1961. G. Cobb, *The Old Churches of London* (1961).

COBB, 1971. G. Cobb, *London City Churches: a brief guide* (3rd edn, 1971).

KISSAN, 1940. B. W. Kissan, 'An Early list of London properties', *Trans. London Middlesex Archaeol. Soc.*, n.s. 8 (1938–40), 57–69.

WALTERS, 1939. H. B. Walters, *London Churches at the Reformation, with an account of their contents* (1939).

Individual churches: a few important articles

CATER, 1922. W. A. Cater, 'The date of the foundation of the church of St. Alphage, London Wall', *Trans. London and Middlesex Archaeol. Soc.*, n.s., 4 (1922), 179–80.

CLAYTON, 1941. P. B. Clayton, 'Saxon discoveries at All Hallows (Barking) Church', *Builder*, 161 (1941), 254–5.

COOK, 1955. G. H. Cook, *Old St. Paul's Cathedral* (1955).

CORCORAN, 1913. B. Corcoran, 'St. Olave's Hart Street, All Hallow's Staining; and the ancient city wall', *Trans. London Middlesex Archaeol. Soc.*, n.s., 2 (1911–13) 225–45.

GRIMES, 1968. See *11*. Grimes 1968.

See index for page references to many City church excavations.

HURST, 1969. See *5*. Hurst 1969, 251.

Excavation of St. Mary Aldermanbury

KENDRICK AND RADFORD, 1943. Sir T. D. Kendrick and C. A. R. Radford, 'Recent discoveries at All Hallows, Barking', *Antiq. J.*, 23 (1943), 14–18.

KISSAN, 1937. B. W. Kissan, 'The earliest mention of Bow Church', *Trans. London Middlesex Archaeol. Soc.*, n.s. 7 (1937), 430–44.

MARSDEN, 1967–8. See *11*. Marsden 1967 and 1968.
Excavation of St. Nicholas Acon, St. Pancras, and St. Michael Bassishaw churches.

MATTHEWS AND ATKINS, 1957. W. R. Matthews and W. M. Atkins (eds) *A History of St. Paul's Cathedral* (1957).

MILLS, 1950. K. Mills, 'St. Peter upon Cornhill in the City, and St. Michael-upon-Cornhill', *T. Eccles. Soc.*, 23 (1950) 162–6.

Southwark

SMITH, 1958. J. T. Smith, 'The Pre-Conquest Minster at Southwark', *Trans. London and Middlesex Archaeol. Soc.*, 19.3 (1958) 174–9.

11 ARCHAEOLOGICAL SITE AND FIND REPORTS

This section includes only multi-period sites and general works on London's archaeology. For work on specific periods and subjects see sections 3, 4, 5, 6 and 10.

DAWE AND OSWALD, 1952. D. Dawe and A. Oswald, *11 Ironmonger Lane: The story of a site in the City of London* (1952).

GRIMES, 1956. W. F. Grimes, 'Excavations in the City of London', *Recent Archaeological Excavations in Britain*, (ed. R. L. S. Bruce-Mitford, 1956), 111–44.

GRIMES, 1968. W. F. Grimes, *The Excavation of Roman and Mediaeval London* (1968).

GUILDHALL, 1961. Guildhall Museum, 'Archaeological finds in the City of London 1960', *Trans. London Middlesex Archaeol. Soc.*, 20 (1959–61), 220–33.

MARSDEN, 1967. P. R. V. Marsden, 'Archaeological finds in the City of London', *Trans. London Middlesex Archaeol. Soc.*, 21.3 (1967), 189–221.

MARSDEN, 1968. P. R. V. Marsden, 'Archaeological finds in the City of London 1965–6', *Trans. London Middlesex Archaeol. Soc.*, 22.1 (1968), 1–17.

MARSDEN, 1969. P. R. V. Marsden, 'Archaeological finds in the City of London 1966–8', *Trans. London Middlesex Archaeol. Soc.*, 22.2 (1969), 1–26.

MARSDEN, 1970. P. R. V. Marsden, 'Archaeological finds in the City of London 1966–9', *Trans. London Middlesex Archaeol. Soc.*, 22.3 (1970), 1–9.

MARSDEN, 1971. P. R. V. Marsden, 'Archaeological finds in the City of London 1967–70', *Trans. London Middlesex Archaeol. Soc.*, 23.1 (1971), 1–14.

OSWALD, 1949a. A. Oswald, 'Finds from London Building Sites 1948', *Archaeol. News Letter*, 11 (1949), 4.

OSWALD, 1949b. A. Oswald, 'Recent London Excavations: a survey of finds', *Archaeol. News Letter*, 9 (1949), 1–3.

VULLIAMY, 1930. C. E. Vulliamy, *The Archaeology of Middlesex and London* (1930).

WADDINGTON, 1930. Q. Waddington, 'Recent light on London's past: a few remarks on the results of excavations in the City in the years 1924–1929', *J. Brit. Archaeol. Ass.*, 2nd s., 36 (1930), 59–80.

Southwark

KENYON, 1959. K. M. Kenyon, *Excavations in Southwark* (Surrey Archaeol. Soc. Research Papers, 5, 1959).

SHELDON, 1971. Harvey Sheldon, 'Excavations at Toppings Wharf, Tooley Street, Southwark', *London Archaeol.*, 1.11 (1971), 252–4.

SAEC, 1972. Southwark Archaeological Excavation Committee, *Southwark's Archaeology: The Final Decade?* (1972).

TURNER, 1967. D. J. Turner, 'Recent Excavations in Southwark and Lambeth', *London Natur.*, 46 (1967), 129–37.

12 SCULPTURE AND INSCRIPTIONS

JAKOBSSON AND MOLTKE, 1941–2. L. Jakobsson and E. Moltke, *Danmarks Runeindskrifter* (Copenhagen 1941–2).
Stone from St Paul's churchyard: items 412, 412a.

MARGUARDT, 1961. H. Marguardt, *Bibliographie der Runeninschriften nach Fundorten, 1* (Göttingen 1961).
London: 93–6,
Thames: 127–9.

OKASHA, 1967. E. Okasha, 'An Anglo-Saxon inscription from All Hallows, Barking-by-the-Tower, London', *Medieval Archaeol.*, 11 (1967), 249–51.

OKASHA, 1971. E. Okasha, *A Handlist of Anglo-Saxon Non-Runic Inscriptions* (Cambridge 1971).

PAGE, forthcoming a. R. I. Page, *An Introduction to English Runes* (forthcoming: Methuen, London).

PAGE, forthcoming b. R. I. Page, *A Handlist of Anglo-Saxon Runic Inscriptions* (forthcoming).

WILSON, 1964. See *4*. Wilson 1964.
Entry concerning two runic inscriptions from the Thames, pp.69,77.

WRIGHT AND HASSALL 1965–72. R. P. Wright and M. S. C. Hassall, 'Roman Britain in 1964/5/6/8/9/70/71, ii: Inscriptions', *J. Roman Stud.*, 55 (1965), 224; *ibid.*, 56 (1966), 224; *ibid.*, 57 (1967), 208; *ibid.*, 59 (1969), 244; *Britannia*, 1 (1970), 312; *ibid.*, 2 (1971), 299–300; *ibid.*, 3 (1972), 357–9.

13 NUMISMATIC EVIDENCE

Bibliographies and Inventories

BROOKE, 1950. G. C. Brooke, *English Coins from the seventh century to the present day* (rev. edn, 1950).

CRAIG, 1953. Sir John Craig, *The Mint: a history of the London Mint from AD 287–1948* (1953).

MATTINGLY AND SYDENHAM, 1933, 1967, 1966, 1951. H. Mattingly and E. A. Sydenham (eds) *The Roman Imperial Coinage*, 5 (1933), 6 (1967), 7 (1966), 9 (1951).

THOMPSON, 1956. J. D. A. Thompson, *An Inventory of British Coin Hoards 600–1500* (Oxford 1956).

BROWN AND DOLLEY, 1971. I. D. Brown and R. H. M. Dolley, *A Bibliography of Coin Hoards of Great Britain and Ireland 1500–1967* (1971).

Roman period

Consult *3*. Bonser 1957, 8: 'Numismatics', 151–62, and *3*. Merrifield 1965, Bibliography, as well as *13*. Mattingly and Sydenham.

COOK, 1968. N. Cook, 'Third century coin moulds from a turret of the Roman wall at the Old Bailey', *Antiq. J.*, 48.2 (1968), 308.

MATTINGLY, 1967. 'The Paternoster Row hoard of barbarous radiates', *Numis. Chron.*, 7.7 (1967), 61–9.

Saxon period

Consult *4*. Bonser 1957, 10: 'Numismatics and Seals', 425–48.

BLUNT AND DOLLEY, 1959. C. E. Blunt and R. H. M. Dolley, 'The Hoard Evidence for the Coins of Alfred', *Brit. Numis. J.*, 29.2 (1959), 220–47.

BOON, 1958. G. C. Boon, 'A note on the Byzantine coins said to have been found at Caerwent', *Bull. Board Celt. Stud.*, 17.3 (1958), 316–9.
Reference to London finds.

BUTLER AND DOLLEY, 1959. V. J. Butler and R. H. M. Dolley, 'New light on the nineteenth-century find of pence of Aethelraed II from St. Martin's-le-Grand', *Brit. Numis. J.*, 29.2 (1959), 265–74.

BUTLER, 1961. V. J. Butler, 'Some misread moneyers of London in the reign of Aethelraed II', *Brit. Numis. J.*, 30.2 (1961), 221–6.

DOLLEY, 1953. R. H. M. Dolley, 'Two unpublished hoards of late Saxon pence in the Guildhall Museum', *Brit. Numis. J.*, 27.2 (1953), 212–3.

DOLLEY, 1956. R. H. M. Dolley, 'A note on the mints of Sudbury and Southwark at the end of the reign of Aethelraed II', *Brit. Numis. J.*, 28 (1956) 264–9.

DOLLEY, 1958. R. H. M. Dolley, 'Three forgotten English finds of pence of Aethelraed II', *Numis. Chron.*, 6th s., 18 (1958), 97–107.

DOLLEY, 1960. R. H. M. Dolley, 'Coin hoards from the London area as evidence for the pre-eminence of London in the later Saxon period', *Trans. London Middlesex Archaeol. Soc.*, 20.2 (1960), 37–50.

DOLLEY, 1964. Michael Dolley, *Anglo-Saxon Pennies* (1964).

DOLLEY, 1965. Michael Dolley, *Viking Coins of the Danelaw and of Dublin* (1965).

DOLLEY, 1966. Michael Dolley, *The Norman Conquest and the English Coinage* (1966).

DOLLEY AND VAN DER MEER, 1959. R. H. M. Dolley and G. van der Meer, 'A die-link between the mints of Dover and London at the end of the reign of Aethelraed II', *Brit. Numis. J.*, 29.2 (1959), 416–7.

HILL, 1958. P. V. Hill, 'Anglo-Frisian trade in the light of eighth century coins', *Trans. London Middlesex Archaeol. Soc.*, 19.3 (1958), 138–46.

KINSEY, 1958. R. S. Kinsey, 'Anglo-Saxon law and practice relating to mints and moneyers, with particular reference to the mints of Chichester, London, Dover and Northampton and the Moneyer(s) Cynsige at Kinsey', *Brit. Numis. J.*, 29.1 (1958), 12–50.

LYON, 1962. C. S. S. Lyon, 'Two notes on the "Last small cross" type of Aethelraed II', *Brit. Numis. J.*, 31 (1962), 49–52.

RIGOLD, 1960. S. E. Rigold, 'The Two Primary Series of Sceattas', *Brit. Numis. J.*, 30 (1960), 6–53.

RIGOLD, 1966. S. E. Rigold, 'The Two Primary Series of Sceattas: Addenda and Corrigenda', *Brit. Numis. J*, 35 (1966), 1ff.

SUTHERLAND, 1948. C. H. V. Sutherland, *Anglo-Saxon Gold Coinage in the light of the Crondall Hoard* (Oxford 1948).

Medieval and Post-medieval
See *13*. Brooke 1950; *13*. Thompson 1956; *13*. Brown and Dolley 1971.

14 OTHER WORKS REFERRED TO IN THE TEXT

ALCOCK, 1971. Leslie Alcock, *Arthur's Britain* (1971).

BIDDLE, 1972. Martin Biddle, 'Excavations at Winchester 1970: ninth interim report', *Antiq. J.*, 52 (1972), 93–131.

BIDDLE, 1974. Martin Biddle (ed.): Frank Barlow, Martin Biddle, Olof von Feilitzen, and D. J. Keene, *Winchester in the early middle ages: an edition and discussion of the Winton Domesday* (Winchester Studies I, Oxford, forthcoming).

BÖHNER, 1966. Kurt Böhner, 'Spätrömische Kastelle und Alamannische Ansiedlungen in der Schweiz', in R. Degen, W. Drach and R. Wyss (eds), *Helvetia Antiqua: festschrift Emil Vogt* (Zürich 1966), 307–16.

BROOKS, 1964. Nicholas Brooks, 'The Unidentified Forts of the Burghal Hidage', *Medieval Archaeol.*, 8 (1964), 74–90.

CUNLIFFE, 1970. Barry Cunliffe, 'The Saxon culture-sequence at Portchester Castle', *Antiq. J.*, 50 (1970), 67–85.

FRERE, 1966. Sheppard Frere, 'The End of Towns in Roman Britain', in J. S. Wacher (ed.), *The Civitas Capitals of Roman Britain* (Leicester 1966), 87–100.

FRERE, 1967. Sheppard Frere, *Britannia* (1967).

FRERE, 1972. Sheppard Frere, *Verulamium Excavations*, I (1972).

HASSALL, 1971. T. G. Hassall, 'Excavations at Oxford 1970: third interim report', *Oxoniensia*, 36 (1971), 1–14.

HAWKES AND DUNNING, 1961. S. C. Hawkes and G. C. Dunning, 'Soldiers and Settlers in Britain: Fourth to Fifth Centuries', *Medieval Archaeol.*, 5 (1961), 1–70.

HERTEIG, 1959. Asbjørn E. Herteig, 'The Excavation of "Bryggen", the old Hanseatic Wharf in Bergen', *Medieval Archaeol.*, 3 (1959), 177–86.

HERTEIG, 1969. Asbjørn E. Herteig, *Kongers Havn og Handels Sete* (Oslo 1969).

HILL, 1969. David Hill, 'The Burghal Hidage: The Establishment of a Text', *Medieval Archaeol.*, 13 (1969), 84–92.

HILL, 1970. David Hill, 'Pont de l'Arche: Frankish influence on the West Saxon burh?', *Archaeol. J.*, 127 (1970), 188–95.

JONES, 1968. M. U. Jones, V. I. Evison and J. N. L. Myres, 'Crop-mark sites at Mucking, Essex', *Antiq. J.*, 48 (1968), 210–30.

KEENE, 1972. D. J. Keene, *The Brooks Area of Medieval Winchester* (unpublished D. Phil. Thesis, Oxford, 1972).

LOMBARD-JOURDAN, 1972. Anne Lombard-Jourdan, 'Oppidum et banlieue: sur l'origine et les dimensions du territoire urbain', *Annales: Economies, Sociétés, Civilisations*, 27 (1972), 373–95.

MORRIS, 1968. John Morris, 'The Date of Saint Alban', *Hertfordshire Archaeol.*, I (1968), 1–8.

MORRIS, 1973. John Morris, *The Age of Arthur* (1973).
This book was unfortunately received too late to be considered in the writing of 4.24–9, but the suggestions put forward seem to be in general agreement with, e.g.. Morris, p.108 ff.

MYRES, 1969. J. N. L. Myres, *Anglo-Saxon Pottery and the Settlement of England* (Oxford 1969).

PAINTER, 1972. K. S. Painter, 'A Late-Roman silver ingot from Kent', *Antiq. J.*, 52 (1972), 84–92.

PETERSSON, 1969. H. Bertil A. Petersson, *Anglo-Saxon Currency: King Edgar's Reform to the Norman Conquest* (Lund 1969).

RADFORD, 1970. C. A. Ralegh Radford, 'The Later Pre-Conquest Boroughs and their Defences', *Medieval Archaeol.*, 14 (1970), 83–103.

RIVET, 1958. A. L. F. Rivet, *Town and Country in Roman Britain* (1958).

ROBERTSON, 1939. A. J. Robertson, *Anglo-Saxon Charters* (Cambridge 1939).

RUSSELL, 1948. J. C. Russell, *British Medieval Population* (Albuquerque 1948).

TAYLOR AND TAYLOR, 1965. H. M. Taylor and Joan Taylor, *Anglo-Saxon Architecture*, I and II (Cambridge 1965).

WEIDEMANN, 1968. K. Weidemann, 'Die Topographie von Mainz in der Römerzeit und dem frühen Mittelalter', *Jahrbuch des Römisch-Germanischen Zentralmuseums Mainz*, 15 (1968), 146–99.

WEIDEMANN, 1970. K. Weidemann, 'Zur Topographie von Metz in der Römerzeit und im frühen Mittelalter', *Jahrbuch des Römisch-Germanischen Zentralmuseums Mainz*, 17 (1970), 147–71.